HANDBOOK ON C++ LANGUAGE

HANDBOOK ON C++ LANGUAGE

By

Sangita Sardana

Lecturer, Dept. of Computer Science

DAV School, Chandigarh

FIREWAL MEDIA

(An Imprint of Laxmi Publications Pvt. Ltd.)

BANGALORE • CHENNAI • COCHIN • GUWAHATI • HYDERABAD
JALANDHAR • KOLKATA • LUCKNOW • MUMBAI • PATNA
RANCHI • NEW DELHI

Published by :

FIREWAL MEDIA

(An Imprint of Laxmi Publications Pvt. Ltd.)
113, Golden House, Daryaganj,
New Delhi-110002
Phone : 011-43 53 25 00
Fax : 011-43 53 25 28
www.laxmipublications.com
info@laxmipublications.com

First Edition: 2011

OFFICES

✆ **Bangalore**	080-26 61 15 61	✆ **Chennai**	044-24 34 47 26
✆ **Cochin**	0484-237 70 04, 405 13 03	✆ **Guwahati**	0361-254 36 69, 251 38 81
✆ **Hyderabad**	040-24 65 23 33	✆ **Jalandhar**	0181-222 12 72
✆ **Kolkata**	033-22 27 43 84	✆ **Lucknow**	0522-220 95 78
✆ **Mumbai**	022-24 91 54 15, 24 92 78 69	✆ **Patna**	09893476827
✆ **Ranchi**	0651-221 47 64		

FC+-3080-175-HANDBOOK ON C++ LANG-SAR C—

Typesetted at : Shubham Composer, N. Delhi. *Printed at :* LB Enterprises, Delhi.

CONTENTS

PREFACE

I am highly glad to present a series on Computer Languages. Writing a book to serve students community, gives a great feeling of satisfaction. Various books on High Level Languages are available in the market but it has been my desire to present such a series on computer languages which could serve the students community in some different manner which could be well acceptable by all. Generally students feel that the books available on the high do not cater to their requirements and there is a dearth of programming examples and graded programs. With the inspiration provided by my students, I have been able to frame a series of four different computer languages C, C++, Java and Visual Basic. Presentation in all the four books is almost on the similar lines.

This treatise covers chapters in uniform manner *i.e.*, from beginning level to advanced level of C ++ language. Advanced topics like Files, Linked Lists, Stacks, queues etc. have been explained in an understandable manner. Each and every topic has been explained with examples and illustrations.

A sufficient number of programming examples has been provided in the book after the topics and as a separate portion in the form of "More Worked Out Examples". Actual screen shots have been given both with program listings and output run.

All efforts have been made to provide the text in an error-free form yet there is a chance within human limitations that some error might have crept in inadvertently. Readers are requested to brought such errors in our notice so that future edition of this book could be improved. The author can be contacted at sangitsardana@yahoo.co.in.

—Author

1

INTRODUCTION TO C++

INTRODUCTION

C++ is a powerful programming language which has been derived from C language. C++ high level retains most of its C heritage. It has adopted basic data types, operations and program structure from C language. C++ was developed in 80's by Bjarne Stroustrup. Simply we can say that C++ is a superset of C language with extensions and improvements and object oriented features included in it.

CHARACTERISTICS OF C++

C++ is an object oriented programming language with a huge library of functions. Its popularity is increasing rapidly and programmers are inclining towards C++ due to its multiple features.

1. C++ is highly flexible language with versatility. It can be used for developing system software viz., operating systems, compilers, editors and data bases.
2. C++ is ideally suited for development of reusable software. This helps in cost reduction of software development.
3. There is no need of re-written software at the time when a computer is upgraded. C++ is a machine independent language.

CHARACTERS USED IN C++

The set of characters used in C++ consists of alphabets, digits and special characters.

The following table represents the characters used in this language.

Letters	A B C D E F G ... X Y Z *a b c d e f g ... x y z*
Numeric Digits	0 1 2 3 4 5 6 7 8 9

Special Characters :

(*i*)	Arithmetic Operators	–, +, *, /, %
(*ii*)	Logical Operators	&, !
(*iii*)	Brackets	( ) { } [ ]
(*iv*)	Relational Operators	< > = #
(*v*)	Other Symbols	:;_ (underscore) > > ?

C++ TOKENS

The group of characters which logically belong together is called Token. Tokens are of following four types.

1. Identifiers   2. Keywords   3. Constants   4. Operators

Identifiers

A program can use various data items with symbolic names in C++. Identifiers refer to the names of functions, arrays, variables, classes etc., created by a programmer. There are certain rules for naming these indentifiers in each language. An identifier, generally, contains symbolic name. These symbolic names are used in various C++ programs. The rules of naming identifiers in C and C++ are similar.

Rules for Naming Identifiers

1. Uppercase letters and lower case letters are distinct. There is a difference between Delhi and DELHI.
2. The name of identifier cannot begin with a digit. 1 DELHI is an invalid name. However, the first character can be selected as an underscore(_).
3. Only alphabetic characters, digits and underscore(_) are permitted in this language.
4. Other special characters are not allowed for naming a variable. White space is also not allowed.
5. The declared key word cannot be used as a variable name.

It is essential to declare variables before their usage in the program. A declaration statement lists the type and number of the variable.

For example

int *i* = 0;	Here i is declared as integer and has been initialized with a value of 0.
char father_name;	Here father_name is character variable.
float mth_sale;	Here mth_sale is a floating point variable.

Keywords

In C++, keywords are reserved identifiers which cannot be used as names for the variables in a program. C++ reserves 63 words for its own use. However the given 48 keywords are mostly and as keywords. The set of C++ keywords has been given in the following list.

asm	double	new	switch
auto	else	operator	template
break	enum	private	this
case	extern	protected	throw
catch	float	public	try
char	for	register	typedef
class	friend	return	union
const	goto	short	unsigned
continue	if	signed	virtual
default	inline	sizeof	void
delete	int	static	volatile
do	long	struct	while

Constants

The items whose values are not changed during the execution of the program are called constants. If an attempt is made to change their values, the program will not successfully execute and generate errors. Each constant is determined by its value and form. C++ has three types of constants.

(*i*) Numeric Constant (*ii*) Character Constant

(*iii*) String Constant

Operators

An operator is a symbol or letter which causes the compiler to take an action and yield a value. An operator acts on different data items/entities called **Operands**.

For example

$x + y$ is an expression in which sign + is an operator which specifies the operation of addition.

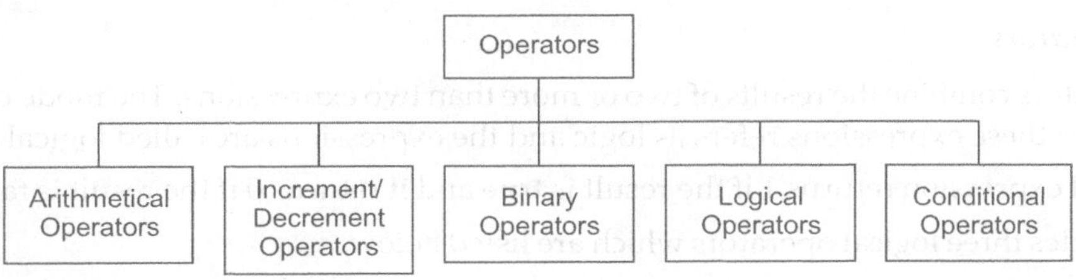

Arithmetical Operators

Arithmetical operators are used to perform various mathematical calculations. The result of an arithmetical expression is a numerical value. An arithmetical expression may be a variable or a constant or a combination of both. These variables or functions are connected with arithmetical operators.

Increment and Decrement Operators

C++ provides ++ and – – operators which are not provided by many other languages. These operators are called increment and decrement operators respectively.

The increment operator ++ adds 1 to its operand.

++ x means $x + 1$

and -- x means $x - 1$

Binary Operators

The Binary operators act upon two operands. The following arithmetical operators require two operands.

Symbols	Meaning	Example
+	Addition or Plus	A + B
–	Subtraction or Minus	A – B
*	Multiplication	A * B
/	Slash or Division	A/B
%	Modulus or Remainder	A%B

Relational Operators

Relational operators are used to determine the relationship between different operands. These are used in the work of comparison also. There are two mathematical expressions and these are connected by a relational operator. The relational expression return 0 if the relation is false and returns 1 if the relation is true. The six relational operators are shown in the following table:

Symbol	Meaning
>	Greater than
<	Less than
> =	Greater than, equal to
< =	Less than, equal to
= =	Equal to
! =	Not equal to

Logical Operators

Logical operators combine the results of two or more than two expressions. The mode of connecting relationship in these expressions refers as logic and the expressions are called logical expressions.

The logical expression returns 1 if the result is true and it returns 0 if the result is false.

C++ provides three logical operators which are listed below.

Symbol	Meaning
!	Logical negation (Logical inverse)
||	Logical OR
&&	Logical AND

STRUCTURE OF A C++ PROGRAM

The following is the structure of a simple C++ Program.

Include Files
Class Declaration
Class Functions Definitions
Main Function Program

```
#include <iostream.h>
main()
    {
    int x,y, sum;                        //Read the values x and y
    cout<<"\Enter the first number:";   //console output and prompt.
    cin>>x;
    cout<<"\Enter the second number:";
    cin>>y;
    sum=x+y;
    cout<<sum<<endl;  //display the output
    return();
    }
```

Explanation

1. A C++ program starts with function called main(). The body of the function is enclosed between curly brackets ({ }). A C++ program can consist of as many functions as required.
2. The explanation written after the characters // is known as comment. Comment plays an important role in development of program. It increases readability of the program.
3. The statement in the program `#include<iostream.h>` is called an **"Include Preprocessor Director."** The symbol # is called hash symbol. The name of the file appears before the start of the program and is known as a **Header File** and has extension *h*.
4. The function **cin** is called console input. It is used with redirection operator >>. It accepts data from the input unit, *i.e.*, keyboard.

   `cin>>x;`

   When this statement is executed, it accepts the value of '*x*' from keyboard.
5. The function cout is called console output. It is used with redirection operator <<. It displays the output on computer screen.

   `cout<<sum<<endl;`

   When this statement is executed, it displays the value (sum) on the screen. endl; is used to show the end of line. It is optional to use endl;
   endl is a manipulator which is frequently used. It has the same effect as character "/*n*", but due to its clarity, endl is preferred.
6. Every statement in C++ should be followed by a semi-colon (`;`). In case this semi-colon is missed, an error message appears while compiling the program.

Importance of iostream.h File

In every C++ program, it is essential to add `iostream.h` header file.

The following sequence is used in the program.

```
#include<iostream.h>
```

This sequence helps the preprocessor to add the contents of `iostream.h` file to the program. This header file should be included at the start of the program that uses input and output statements. The header file `iostream.h` contains declaration for the identifier cout and for the operator <<.

The cin Operator(>>)

The cin operator is used to get input from the standard input device *i.e.,* keyboard. When you write C++ programs and use cin, you do not know the values of the input until the program is run. You can enter the values from the keyboard after the program is run. You can also fill the values using assignment statement such as $i = 15$; The difference between an assignment statement and cin operator is that the value of input is known in case of assignment statement whereas it is not known in case of cin operator.

Syntax

```
cin>>values;
```

```
Look at the following program:
//INTRO.CPP
#include<iostream.h>
main( )
{
    int x,y;
    cout<<"Enter one value=";
    cin>>x;                          //input the value of x
    cout<<"Enter second value=";
    cin>>y;                          //input the value of y
    cout<<"The sum is=" <<x+y<<endl;
    return0;
}
```

When you will run the above program, computer will ask you to input the values of x and y.

Enter one value = 10

Enter second value = 20

The sum is = 30

The cout Operator(<<)

The << operator is used to obtain the output on a standard output device. This device may be screen of the monitor.

Syntax

```
cout<<data;
```

Examples

```
cout<<"I am a student of B.Com. class";
cout<<"I read in S.D. College";
```

CASCADING OF I/O OPERATORS

The input and output redirection operators are called I/O operators and written as cin >> and cout<<. When a second I/O redirection operator is written after the first I/O redirection operator, it is called cascading of I/O operator.

```
cout <<"The sum of variables"
     <<a<< "and"
     <<b<< "is"<<a+b;
cin >>"enter the first number">>a;
cout <<"the first number"<<a;
```

The external file `iostream.h` provides input and output functions.

Multiple use of input (>>) and output (<<) operators in one statement is called cascading of I/O operators.

The setw() Manipulator

The `setw()` manipulator is used along with output operator << to display the output. It stands for set width.

This manipulator `setw(n)` puts the output in a specified zone of n characters.

Syntax

setw(int *n*)

The default width is zero.

For example

```
cout<<set(5) <<50;
```

The above line segment will set a zone of 5 columns. The number 50 will be displayed as

```
50
-----
```

Illustration: *The following program illustrates the use of setw ( ) manipulatior.*

Solution.

```
#include<iostream.h>
# include<iomanip.h>
main()
{
    int x,y;
    x = 200;
    y = 400;
cout<<setw(5)<<x<<setw(5)<<y>>endl;
cout<<setw(6)<<x<<setw(6)<<y>>endl;
}
```

The output of the program will be as under:

```
200 400
200 400
```

ERROR MESSAGE

While writing C++ programs, various errors may occur. These errors have been shown in the following figure.

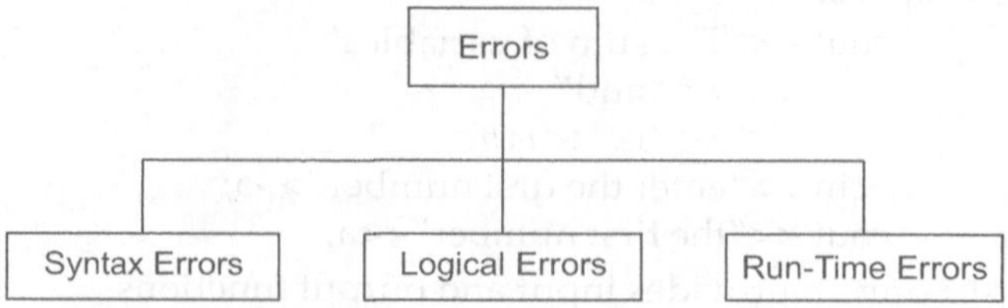

Syntax Errors

Syntax errors occur due to violation of syntax rules in C++. Programs having syntax errors do not execute. It is necessary to remove these errors. These errors can be located by compilers.

Logical Errors

Logical errors occur due to wrong use of logics, *i.e.*, formulae. Programs having logical errors can execute and compile, but the result obtained is erroneous. **To locate these errors** the program writer has to study the program carefully. These errors cannot be located by compilers.

Run-Time Errors

Run-time errors occur when the operation can not be performed during execution. Programs having **Run-time errors** can compile but can not produce meaningful results.

Illustration: *Write a C++ program which finds the square of an integer.*

Solution:

```
//This program finds the square of an integer
#include<iostream.h>
main( )
    {
        int number;
        cout<<"\n Enter the number:"
        cin>>number;
        square = number * number;
        cout<<"\n Square of the number ="<<square;
        return 0;
    }
```

1. `//This program finds square of the number.`
2. `#include file;`
3. `main()`
4. `{`
5. `int number;`

```
cout<<"\n  Enter  the  number:";
cin>>number;
square=number*number;
cout<<"\n  Square  of  the  number="<<square;
return  0;
```

This program does not compile successfully. The compiler shows the following error messages;

Error: Expression syntax in function main()

Error: Undefined syntax "square" in main function()

1. The actual error is in the following statement:

   ```
   cout<<"\Enter  the  number:"
   ```

   In this statement, the semi-colon is missing.
2. The second message points error in the following statement:

   ```
   square  =  number*number;
   ```

   The error message states that the identifier square has not been declared in the program. You will have to define it as int number, square;

USE OF EDITOR

The editor allows the user to type and edit the program. The program which has been created by the help of an editor is called a **Source Program** or **Source Code**.

Illustration: *If you have turbo C++ program, then the following steps can be used:*

1. The screen of the computer shows the following:

   C:\>CD TC ↵

   C:\TC>CD BIN ↵
2. Invoke Turbo C++ by entering TC.

   C:\TC\BIN>TC ↵

   After executing the above command, you can Load a File in the memory. You have to give it .CPP extension.
3. You can type the program in text window.
4. Save the program by pressing [F2] key. For saving, you can choose a suitable name, say, INTRO.CPP. The extension CPP indicates that "INTRO" is a C++ program. If you don't give extension of .CPP to that program, on saving, it will automatically have. C extension. CPP means C Plus Plus.

COMPILATION

When you have written the C++ program, it is compiled with the help of compiler. A compiler is nothing but a program which translates the source program in to machine executable form.

INTRO.CPP has to be compiled and then to be linked to obtain INTRO.EXE. The source program after compilation is called object program.

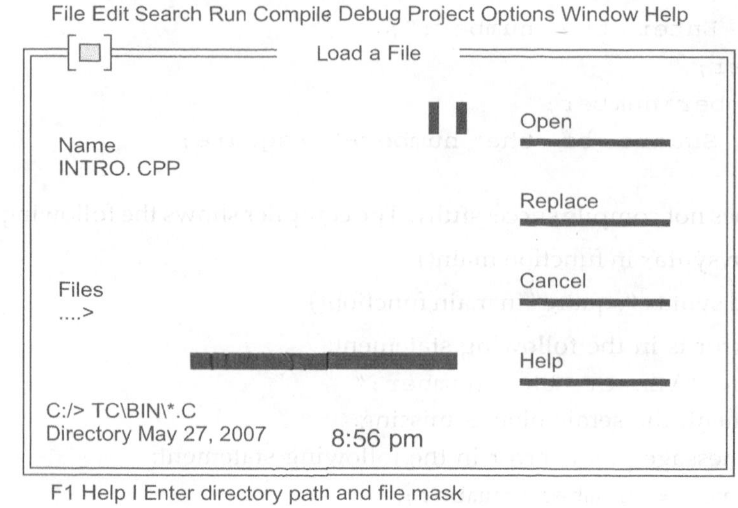

After typing the name you will reach at the Text window.

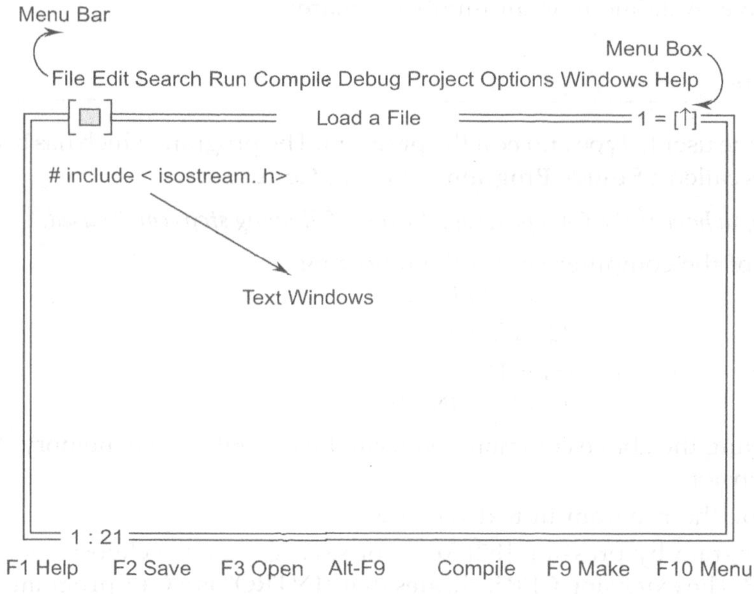

Linking

Mostly the programs use built-in functions. These are also called library functions. The linker is used to link these functions with the object program. After linking, the object program is called Final Executable Program or Module.

Execution

The final executable program can be executed to obtain the output.

SOME MORE WORKED-OUT EXAMPLES

1. Find the syntax errors in the following program.

```
1. #include<iostream.h>
2. void Main()
3. {
4. const MAX = 0;
5. int a,b;
6. cin<<a>>b;
7. if (a > b) MAX = a;
8. for(x=0,x<MAX;x++)
9. cout<<x;
10. }
```

Solution. In line number 2, Main() should be as main()
The line number 6 should be as `cin>>a>>b;`
In line number 8, x = 0, should be as x = 0;

2. Find the syntax errors in the following program.

```
1. #include<iostream.h>
2. void main()
3. {
4. int x,y;cin>>x;
5. for(x=0;x<5,++x)
6. cout y else cout<<x<<y;
7. }
```

Solution.

1. In line number 6-cout y should be as cout<<*y*;
2. else is without if
3. line number 5 should be as for(*x*=0;*x*<5;++*x*)

3. Find the syntax errors.

```
#include<iostream.h>
Main()
{
int ch=9,sch=90;
char S[2,2];
if ch<=9
cout<<ch;
for(int y=0;<2;y++)
for(int y=0;y<2;y++)
{
```

```
11. if(y==0)S[x][y]="A";
12. else S[x][y]='B';
13. cout>>S[x][y];
14. }
15.
16. getch();
17. }
```

Solution.

Line	No. Error
5.	char S[2,2]; should be as char S[2][2];
6.	if ch<=9 should be if (ch<=9)
11.	"A"; should be as 'A';
13.	cout>>S[x][y]; should be as cout<<S[x][y];
16.	getch(); function is available in <conio.h>file. The file has not been included in the beginning.
4.	The integer variable sch has been given a value but not used anywhere.
2.	Main() should be as main()

2

DATA TYPES IN C++

INTRODUCTION

To write C++ programs, a programmer, is required to have ample knowledge of data types, variables and constants.

C++ provides a set of predefined data types.

CONCEPTS OF DATA TYPES

Data used in computer is of various types. It may include integers, characters, strings etc.

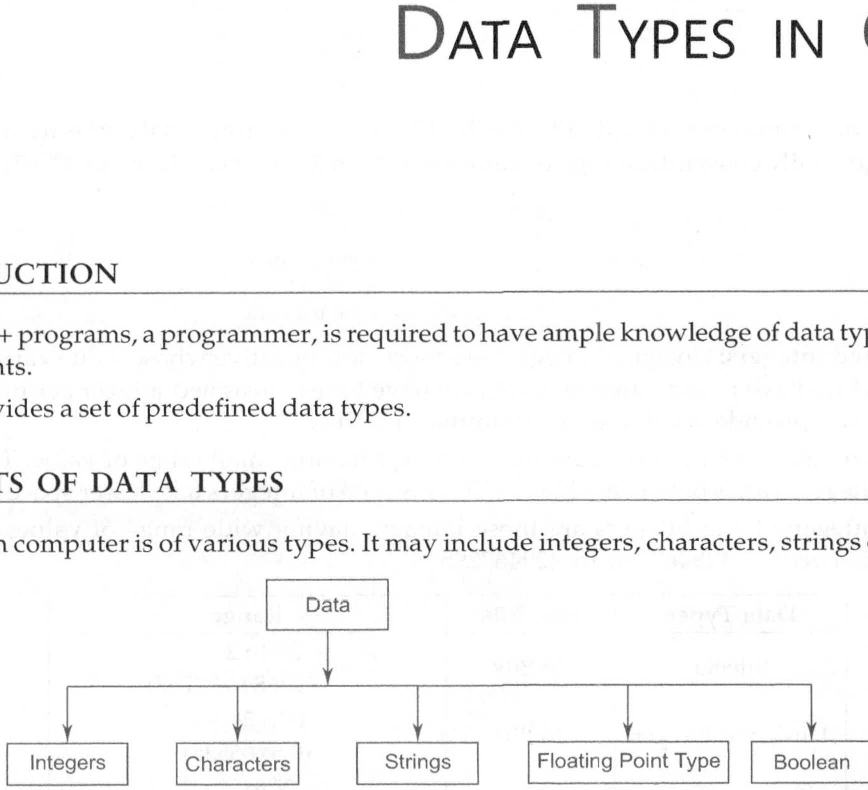

A programmer, while writing programs, has to deal with various types of data; hence it becomes necessary that the programming language should facilitate the programmer in all types of data. The programming language C++ provides all data types.

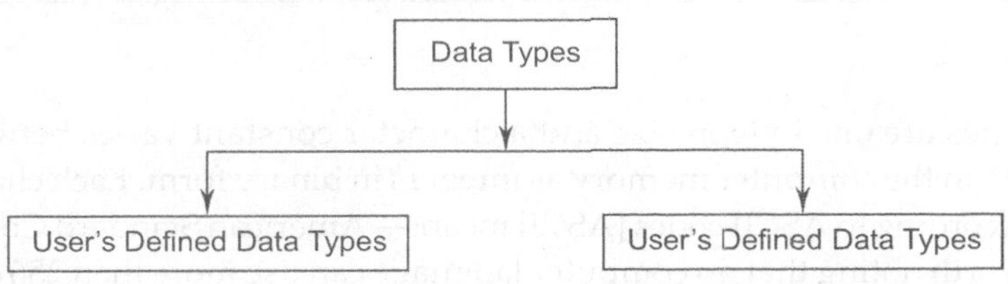

Built-in Data Types

These data types are the part of C++ language. These are also known as standard data-types.

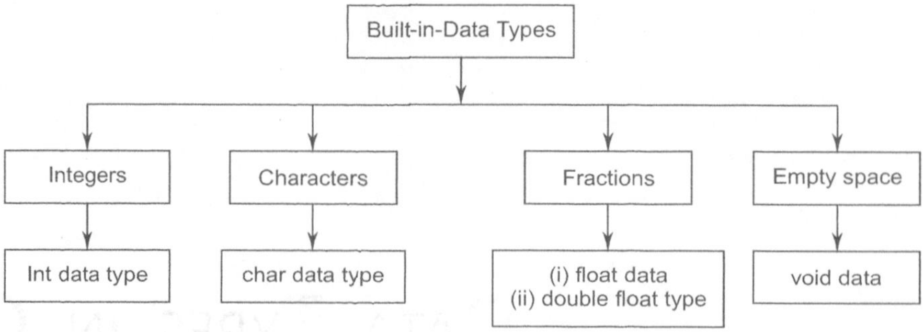

Integers

Integers are whole numbers such as 5, 12, 27, – 5, – 12, – 27, etc. No fractional part is used in integers. Integers are generally constants. Range of values is -2^{15} to $2^{15}-1$(*i.e.* – 32768 to 32767)

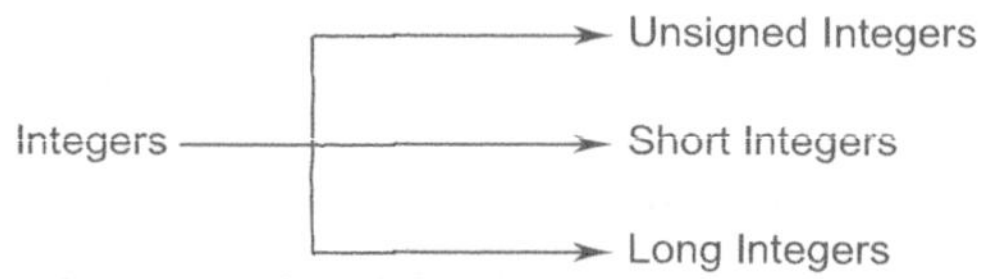

(*i*) **Unsigned Integers:** Unsigned integers are those non-negative whose value varies from 0 to 65535. If we have to use value of 32785, we have to use unsigned integer because ordinary integer can provide a value to a maximum of 32767.

(*ii*) **Short Integers:** Short integers are those integers having small range of value. The value of these integers varies between – 128 to 127. This type of integers take lesser space for storage.

(*iii*) **Long Integers:** Long integers are those integers having wide range of values. The value varies between – 429467296 to 429467295.

Data Types	Size Bits	Range
Integer	16 Bits	-2^{15} to $2^{15}-1$ (– 32768 to 32767)
Unsigned Integer	16 Bits	0 to $2^{16}-1$ (0 to 65535)
Short Integer	8 Bits	-2^{7} to $2^{7}-1$ (– 128 to 127)
Long Integer	32 Bits	-2^{32} to $2^{32}-1$ – 4294967296 to 4294967295

Character Types

Character (char) types are one byte in size and a character constant varies between 0 to 255. The characters are stored in the computer memory as integers in binary form. Each character is assigned a particular value according to ASCII codes [ASCII means—American Standard Code for Information Interchange]. It is worth noting that no computer language can use more than 256 characters [A to Z, numbers, punctuation marks etc.], therefore, these characters are assigned coding from 0-255.

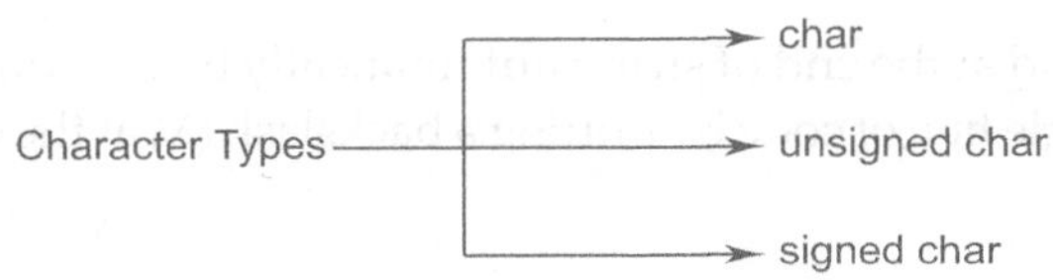

Character Types	Size	Range
char	1 Byte	-2^7 to $2^7 - 1$ (– 128 to 127)
unsigned char	1 Byte	0 to $2^8 - 1$ (0 to 255)
signed char	1 Byte	-2^7 to $2^7 - 1$ (– 128 to 127)

Special Printing Characters

Characters can be written by writing the character in single quotes. But some characters are written in C++ program by using Escape, Carriage Return, Tab characters. C++ compiler recognizes these characters for formatting.

Escape character (\) changes the meaning of the character which follows it, *e.g.*, the character b indicates the letter b but when it is preceded by escape character, it means Back Space.

Character	Meaning
\n	New Line
\t	Horizontal Tab
\v	Vertical Tab
\b	Back Space
\\	Back Slash
\"	Double Quotes
\'	Single Quote
\?	Question Mark
\r	Carriage Return
\f	Form Feed

String

String is a series of characters.

The string is enclosed within double quotes. A string is used to write or store messages.

"HELLO"

The "HELLO" is a string and the characters of a string are stored in sequential locations.

H
E
L
L
O
/φ ⟶ Null character

The null character is added at the end of string automatically by the compiler. String literals can be extended to more than a single line of code by putting a backslash (\) at the end of each unfinished line.

"String is expressed\

in two lines"

Floating-Point Constants

(Float Data Type)

A fractional number is a floating point number. Decimal in a number means that it is a floating number.

A floating point constant may bear +ve or –ve sign. In case no sign is used, the number is treated to be as positive. Floating form provides greater range of integers between –ve to +ve.

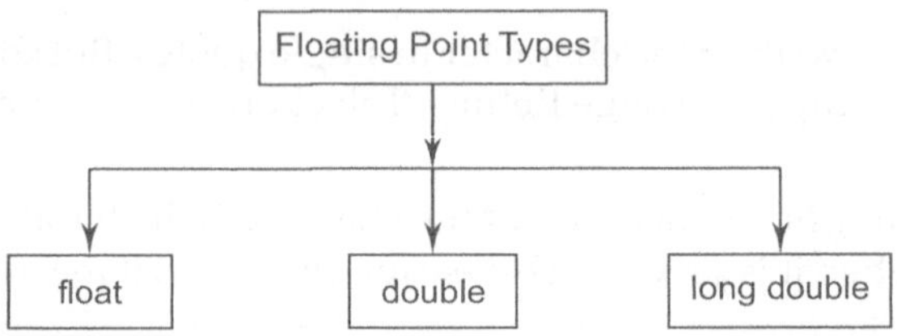

Type	Size	Range
float	4 Bytes	3.4×10^{-38} to 3.4×10^{38}
double	8 Bytes	1.7×10^{-308} to 1.7×10^{308}
long double	10 Bytes	3.4×10^{-4932} to 3.4×10^{4932}

Some valid floating point/constants

(*i*) 5.0 (with decimal)

(*ii*) + 0.1832 (with +ve sign)

(*iii*) – 12.18 (with –ve sign)

Invalid floating point constants

(*i*) 12 (fractional portion is absent)

(*ii*) ± 20.123 (Both signs not allowed)

(*iii*) + 20.123 (Blank space after + sign not allowed)

(*iv*) – 20.123 (Blank space after – sign not allowed)

(*v*) 20,23.1516 (comma not allowed)

(*vi*) 20,23.1516 (Blank space between digits not allowed)

We have observed that range of floating-point constants has been shown in the terms of power having base 10.

Floating-point constants written in this form are called to be in **exponent** form (E-notation)

This notation is also called standard form.

91360000 ⟶ 9.136×10^{6}		
0.9136 ⟶ 9.136×10^{-1}		Standard form or
0.00009136 ⟶ 9.136×10^{-5}		Scientific Notation

Representation in Exponent Form in C++

9.136×10^6	can be written as 9.136E6
9.136×10^{-6}	can be written as 9.136E–6
9.136×10^6	can be written as 9.136E+6
9.136×10^6	can also be written as 9.136E06

———— E ————
Left Part   Right Part

Left part is called mantissa.

Right part is called exponent.

9.136E is invalid notation because exponent is absent.

E6 is invalid notation because mantissa is absent.

Double Data: Type occupies double memory than that of **Float Types**. This stores floating point number with much larger range.

Boolean Literals

There are only two valid Boolean values; true and false. These can be expressed in C++ by using the Boolean literals `true` and `false`.

Defined constants (# define)

You can define your own names for constants that you use very often without having to resort to memory-consuming variables, simply by using the `# define` preprocessor directive.

Format

```
#define identifier value
```

For example:

```
    #define PI 3.14159265
    #define NEWLINE '\n'
```

This defines two new constants: `PI` and `NEWLINE`. Once they are defined, they can be used in the rest of the code as if they were any other regular constant, for example:

```
//defined constants: calculate circumference 31.4159

#include<iostream>

#define PI 3.14159
#define NEWLINE '\n'

int main()
{
  double r=5.0;                    //radius
  double circle;
```

```
    circle=2*PI*r;
    cout<<circle;
    cout<<NEWLINE;

    return 0;
}
```

In fact the only thing that the compiler preprocessor does when it encounters `#define` directives is to literally replace any occurrence of their identifier by the code to which they have been defined (`3.14159265` and `'\n'` respectively).

The `#define` directive is not a C++ statement but a directive for the preprocessor; therefore, it assumes the entire line as the directive and does not require a semicolon (;) at its end. If you append a semicolon character (;) at the end, it will also be appended in all occurrences within the body of the program that the preprocessor replaces.

Declared constants (const)

With the `const` prefix you can declare constants with a specific type in the same way as you would do with a variable:

```
    const int width = 100;
    const char tab = '\t';
```

Here, `width` and `tab` are two typed constants. They are treated just like regular variables except that their values cannot be modified after their definition.

USER'S DEFINED DATA TYPES

User has the facility in the programming language to create data types according to his own needs. Not only he can use built-in data types but also data types as per his own needs. These types contain array, function, pointers, constants, classes etc.

Array

An Array is a collection of fixed-size finite number of objects, data value that belong to the same type. An array is a collection of data storage locations. Each of the locations holds same type of data. The Storage Location is called an element or component of the array. The individual element within the array is called **subscript**.

The subscript is the number of elements in the array surrounded by square brackets [ ].

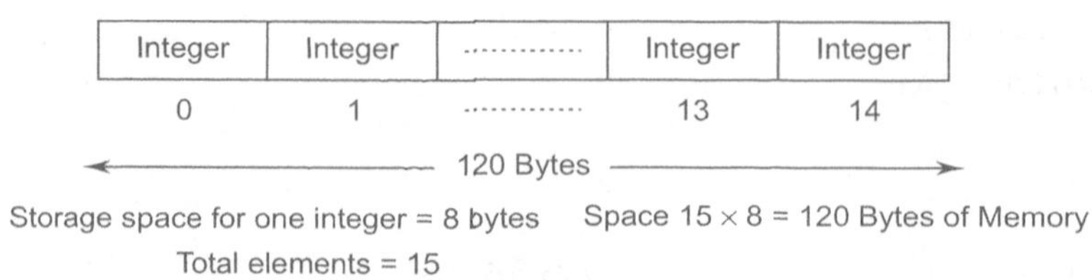

(Declaring an Array)

Array elements are counted from 0.

In the above figure 15 elements are numbered from [0] to [14].

An array may be one-dimensional, two-dimensional or multi-dimensional depending up the specification of elements.

Class

A class is a collection of objectives. It is a user-defined aggregate data type. A class may be defined as a group of objects with same operations and attributes. The 'class' is a keyword in C++ programming. The user deals with classes instead of dealing with various individual objects.

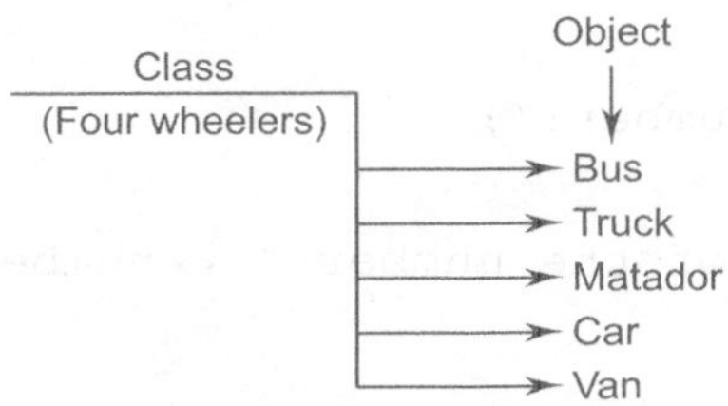

The objects belonging to a class are called instances of the class.

Pointer

A pointer is a variable which holds a memory address within.

Each variable is located at a particular position in the memory which is known as **Address.** The address can be stored in a pointer. A program accesses the value in the address stored in the pointer by using indirection operator.

General Syntax

`type*ptr;` (ptr is the name of pointer)

In a program, pointers are used for the following tasks:

(*i*) Managing data on free storage locations of the memory.
(*ii*) Passing variables by reference to functions.
(*iii*) Accessing class member data and functions.

Function

A function is a subprogram that acts on data and returns a value. A function can be invoked from the other parts of the program.

Every C++ program contains one function, *i.e.*, `main()`. When the program starts, main() automatically becomes active and can call other functions. A function can perform a specific task for the programmer. It is better to use multiple functions in the lengthy task.

Functions are of two types:

(*i*) Built-in functions
(*ii*) User-defined functions

Example

This program illustrates the use of a function.

```
#include<iostream.h>
#include<conio.h>
#include<math.h>
   float square(float);      //Function declaration
   main()
   {
     clrscr();
     float number;
     cout<<"\n Enter Number:";
        cin>>number;
     cout<<"\n Square of the number=" <<number<<square(number);
     return 0;
   }
     float square(float x)
     {
       return x*x;
     }
```

Reference

A reference is an alias, *i.e.*, an alternative name for an object. As soon as a reference is created, the program initializes it with the name of previously defined object. This object is called **Target**. Any change(s) made in the reference directly affects/affect the Target.

General Syntax

type & someRef = someVariable;

someRef is a reference to the variable that is initialized to refer to someVariable.

Example: *If **Product** is declared as a reference to the variable Multiplication, then both Product and Multiplication represent the same variable. Both of these can be used interchangeably.*

```
int product;
int &product = multiplication;
multiplication = 256;
cout<<"\n Product="<<product;
cout<<"\n Multiplication="<<multiplication:
Output will be ———→ Product=256
                     Multiplication=256
```

Variable

As the name suggests, a variable is a quantity which varies during a program execution. In C++, a variable is a location where the information is stored. This locations exists in computer memory where the value/information can be stored and in case of need it can be retrieved.

Variable					
Name Memory					
Memory Address	151	152	153	154	155

Depending upon the size of variable, it can occupy one or more memory address.

Variables can be created by any combination of Letters without spaces. Variable name may be short or descriptive but a descriptive variable name makes it easier to understand the flow of the program. Some keywords are reserved in C++ and cannot be used as variable name like—if, while, main, for. We can create more than one variable of the same type in a single statement. This can be done by the following syntax:

Syntax

```
type varname, VarName;
```

Rules for Creating Variables

1. A variable may consist one or more than one letters, numerals and underscore (_).
2. The first letter of the variable name should not be any numeral. It can be any alphabet or underscore.
3. Try to use meaningful variable names.
4. Do not use keywords as variable names.
5. Obtain the list of Reserved keywords of C++. Compiler manual of the computer provides a complete list of the reserved keywords.
6. No blank space is allowed in a variable name.
7. C++ is a case sensitive. Two words may be different for it. It can distinguish between uppercase and lowercase letters.

delhi	DELHI
deLHi	Delhi

   All are different variables.
8. Try to use the same style of using the variable names throughout the program.
9. Use of any special character is not allowed in the variable name.

de*+lhi is invalid variable name.

Variable may be built-in data type or user-defined type. A variable name is an identifier and all rules pertaining to identifiers apply on the variables.

General Syntax of declaration.

```
data-type list;
```

Following are some examples of declaration of variables:

1. int value;
2. double salary, bonus, increment;
3. int principal, rate, time;
4. unsigned long int number, cube of number;

5. unsigned short int odd;
6. float a, sum;

It is clear from the above examples when two or more identifiers belong to the same data type, we can use single declaration statement. Identifiers are separated by comma. The main advantage of declaration of variables is that the programmer is not at compulsion to trace back the beginning of the program to ascertain the data type linked with these identifiers. A variable can be declared anywhere in the C++ program.

The following are valid variable declarations:

1. `int age;`
   `age=25;`
2. `int weight;`
   `weight=60;`
3. `int height;`
   `int age;`
   `int weight;`
   `height= 167;`
   `age=25;`
   `weight=50;`

Illustration: *The following program illustrates that a variable can be declared anywhere in the program.*

```
#include<iostream.h>
void main()
 {      int a;
        int b;
        a=25;
        b=35;
        int c;       //declaration of variable at new place.
        c=a+b;
        cout<<"Sum of numbers is="<<c;
        return 0;
}
```

3

OPERATORS AND EXPRESSIONS IN C++

OPERATORS

An operator is a symbol or letter which causes the compiler to take an action and yield a value. An operator acts on different data items/entities called Operands.

For example

$a + b$ is an expression in which sign + is an operator which specifies the operation of addition. C++ provides various operators.

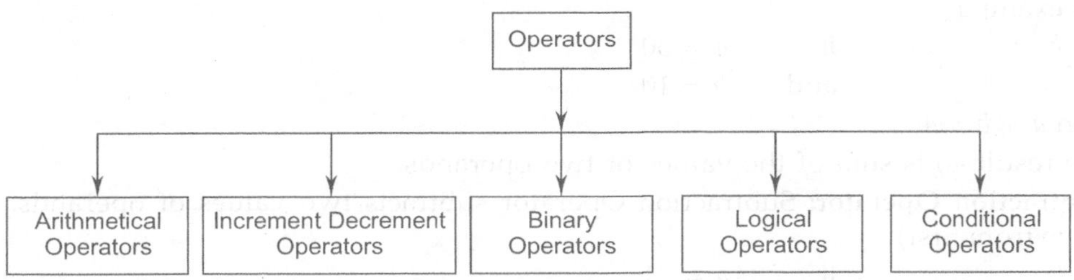

Arithmetical Operators

Arithmetical operators are used for various mathematical calculations. The result of an arithmetical expression is a numerical value. An arithmetical expression may be a variable or a constant or a combination of both. These variables or functions are connected with arithmetical operators.

Arithmetical operators are of following types.

(*i*) Unary Arithmetic Operator

(*ii*) Binary Arithmetic Operator

Unary Arithmetic Operator

The unary operator needs only one operand. It may be + or –.

For example $-a$, $+b$ use unary operator (negative and positive) (*a*) **Unary + :** The operator unary + must have arithmetic type and the result comes in the value or argument.

If $a = 10$ then $+a$ means 10

a means $+10$

and $+a$ means $+10$

If $a = -10$ then $+a$ means -10

(b) **Unary – :** The operator unary – (minus) must have arithmetic type and the result comes in negative.

If $a = -20$ then $-a$ means 20

$-a$ means -20

Binary Arithmetic Operators

The Binary Arithmetic Operators act upon two operands. The following arithmetical operators require two operands.

Symbols	Meaning	Example
+	Addition or Plus	A + B
–	Subtraction or Minus	A – B
*	Multiplication	A * B
/	Slash or Division	A/B
%	Modulus or Remainder	A % B

(*i*) **Addition Operator:** Addition Operator adds two values of operands.

For example

$a + b$ If $a = 30$

and $b = 10$

then $a + b = 40$

The result 40 is sum of the values of two operands.

(*ii*) **Subtraction Operator:** Subtraction Operator subtracts two values of operands. (Second value from first)

$a - b$ if $a = 21$

$b = 6$

then $a - b = 15$

(*iii*) **Multiplication Operator:** Multiplication Operator + multiplies the values of operands.

$a * b$ If $a = 9$

$b = 6$

then $a * b = 54$

(*iv*) **Division Operator:** Division Operator / divides the first operand by the second.

For example a/b

If $a = 75$

$b = 5$

$a/b = 15$

(*v*) **Modulus Operator:** Modulus Operator % finds the remainder when first operand is divided by the second.

For example a % b

If $a = 44$

$b = 6$

a % $b = 2$ because on dividing 44 by 6 we get 2 as remainder.

This type of operator is applicable only when two operands are of integer type.

Increment and Decrement Operator

C++ provides ++ and – – operator which are not provided by the some languages. These operators are called increment and decrement operators.

The increment operator ++ adds 1 to its operand.

++ a means $a + 1$ $\quad$ a++ means $a + 1$

and – – a means $a - 1$ $\quad$ a– – means $a - 1$

These operators exist in 2 types.

(*i*) Prefix

(*ii*) Postfix

Prefix means before its operand and postfix means after its operand.

$\left.\begin{matrix} ++x \\ --x \end{matrix}\right]$ Prefix Type $\quad$ $\left.\begin{matrix} x++ \\ x-- \end{matrix}\right]$ Postfix Type

Example

1. Prefix Increment Operator

   Consider the following program segment

```
..................
..................
i = 20;
net_value = + + i * 8;
cout<<"\net value is:"<<net_value;
..................
..................
```

   The output of that program will be

   net_value = 168 *i.e.* (21 × 8) (First increment the value)

2. Postfix Increment Operator

   Consider the following program segment

```
..................
..................
i = 20;
net_value = i++ *8;
cout<<"\net value is:"<<net_value;
..................
..................
```

   The output of that program will be

   i = 20;

   net_value = 160 *i.e.* (20 × 8); (First use the value)

Evaluate the following expressions (Given $a = 10, b = 8$) (∵ ++*i* means *i*)

(*i*) *a* % *b*++ (*ii*) ++*a* – *b*– –

(*iii*) *a*++ – *b*– – (*iv*) *a*– – + *b*++

Solution.

(*i*) 10%(8++) = 10%8 = 2

(*ii*) ++10 –(8– –) = 11 – 8 = 3

(*iii*) 10++ –(8– –) = 10 – 8 = 2

(*iv*) 10– – +(8++) = 10 + 8 = 18.

Unary Operators	Binary Operators
The operators which act upon a single operand are called unary operators.	The operators which require two operands for their action are called binary operators.
They are pre-increment and post increment(++)	They are mathematical operators and relational operators.

Relational Operators

Relational operators are used to determine the relationship between different operands. These are used in the work of comparison also. There are two mathematical expressions and these are connected by a relational operator. The relational expression returns 0 if the relation is false and returns 1 if the relation is true. Relational operators have been shown in the following table.

Symbol	Meaning
>	Greater than
<	Less than
>=	Greater than, equal to
<=	Less than, equal to
==	Equal to
!=	Not equal to

The following table will help you in understanding the relational operators and their results.

Result							
a	*b*	*a*>*b*	*a*<*b*	*a*>=*b*	*a*<=*b*	*a*==*b*	*a*!=*b*
1	0	1	0	1	0	0	1
0	1	0	1	0	1	0	1
1	1	0	0	1	1	1	0
4	5	0	1	0	1	0	1

In the above table, the Result part of table contains 0s and 1s.

0 means false.

1 means true.

Example 1. *Evaluate the following expressions on the basis of declarations given below.*

int x = 0, a = 5, b = – 5;

1. $x < = a > = b$
2. $x > a$

Solution.

1. The expression $x < = a > = b$ is correct
   Since $x <= a$
   and $x >= b$
   Substituting the values of these variables, we get the value 1 which means the expression is true.
2. The expression $x > a$ is not correct because $x = 0$ and $a = 5$, we get the result as 0 which means the expression is false.

Example 2. *If a = 2 and b = 5; calculate the following expressions.*

1. $a! = b$
2. $a < b$
3. $a + b < = b$

Solution.

1. The expression is true because $a = 2$ and $b = 5$. These values are not equal. Hence we get the result 1 (True).
2. The expression is true because the value of a is less than that of b. Result is 1 (true).
3. The expression is false because the value of $a + b = 2 + 5 = 7$ and it is greater than the value of b. Hence the result is 0 (false).

Logical Operators

Logical operators combine the results of two or more than two expressions. The mode of connecting relationship in these expressions refers as logic and the expressions are called logical expressions.

The logical expression returns 1 if the result is true and it returns 0 if the result is false.

C++ provides three logical operators which are listed below.

Symbol	Meaning
!	Logical negation (Logical inverse)
||	Logical OR
&&	Logical AND

Logical Operator (!)

The logical operator has logical negation. It, has higher precedence over the remaining logical operators. This operator is also called logical NOT operator. This works on single operand and can be referred to as unary operator. To negate an expression, the expression should be enclosed in parentheses.

The ! operator negates the real value of the expression. If the expression is true. ! expression becomes false and if the expression is false, ! expression becomes true.

⇒ If the expression is a zero, ! expression is 1

and if the expression is non-zero, ! expression is 0

Example

! (12) is a non-zero expression but it results into 0 (false)

! (12 > 8) is a true expression because 12 > 8, but it results into 0 (false)

The Logical OR (||)

The logical OR expression (| |) combines two expressions. If both the operands are false, the logical OR operation is false. The logical OR expression results into 1 (true) if either of the operands is true.

Operand 1	Operand 2	Operand 3
False	False	0 (zero)
True	True	1 (non-zero)
False	True	1 (non-zero)
True	False	1 (non-zero)

Example. *Evaluate the following expressions;*

Given that

int i = 0, x = 5, y = – 10;
float a = 3.0, b = 1.0;

1. $x + y \; || \; !i$
2. $a * b < i + x \; || \; y$

Solution.

1. By putting the values of variables in the expression $x + y \; || \; !i$ we get the result as 1(true) (Because $x + y = 5 + (-10) = -5$ and $i = 0$)
2. By substituting the values of various variables, we get the result as 1 (true). This can be understood in the following way.

$a * b = 3$

and $i + x = 5$

$y = -10$

$\Rightarrow$ $a * b < i + x$

The Logical Operator AND (&&)

The logical OR operator (&&) connects two expressions to make them as a single expression. If both the original expressions are true, the resulting expression results a value 1(true) otherwise false.

Operand 1 *a*	Operand 2 *b*	Result *a && b*
0	0	0
1	1	1
0	1	0
1	0	0

Examples

(5 = = 3) && (8 = = 8) It results into 0 (false) because the first expression is false.

(5 = = 5) && (8 = = 8) It results into 1 (true) because both the expressions are true.

5 > 9 && 6 > 2 It results into 0 (false) because the first expression is false.

Conditional Operator

Conditional Operator is also called ternary operator. It is represented by (?:). This is the only operator in C++ which takes three terms (Operands) and returns a value. The value of an expression using this operator is the value of either its second operand or third operand, depending upon the value of first operand. However, ternay operator is sometimes a confused control structure.

(expression 1)? (expression 2): (expression 3);

If expression 1 is true, the result of the operator is the value of expression 2; otherwise it results in the value of expression 3.

The first operand is a test condition, the second and the third operands represent the final value of the expression and out of these values, one is selected depending upon the value of first operand.

Example 1. If $a = 5$

$b = 10$;

$x = (a < b)\ ?\ a : b;$

The above statement reads if a is less than b, then output the value of a otherwise b. The result of the above program segment will be 5.

Example 2. *Rewrite the following using Ternary operator.*

if (income <= 10000)

tax = 0;

else

tax = 12;

Solution. Income <= 10000 ? 0 : 12

Or it can be written as

Income < = 10000 ? 0 : 10000*0.12

(assuming that tax rate is 12% if the income is greater than Rs. 10000)

PRECEDENCE OF OPERATORS

Precedence and Associativity are the two important properties of operators.

Precedence is the order in which a program performs/evaluates the operations in a formula. All operators have precedence value. An operator with higher precedence value is evaluated first than an operator having lower precedence value. Multiplication has higher precedence than addition.

Consider the following expression

$x = 5 + 4 * 6;$

The value of this expression is 29 and not 54. Multiplication has been performed first in this expression. The operand 4 is bound with multiplication operator rather than addition operator. Grouping of operands with operators, occur in two manners.

(*i*) left to right manner

(*ii*) right to left manner.

Left to right associativity means that evaluation is performed from left to right. The compiler starts from the left side. Similarly, right to left associativity means the evaluation from right to left.

When two mathematical operators have the same precedence, they are performed in left to right manner.

$$x = 2 + 3 + 4 * 5 + 6 * 7;$$

The operation starts from multiplication in the following manner.

$$x = 2 + 3 + 20 + 42;$$

Now the addition operator starts from left to right.

$$x = 5 + 20 + 42;$$
$$x = 25 + 42;$$
$$x = 67;$$

Assignment operators are evaluated in right to left order.

The order of precedence can be changed by using parentheses in the expression.

The variables/items in the expression within parentheses are evaluated first than any of the other mathematical operators.

Operator Precedence

Operator Precedence

Operator	Associativity	
( ) [ ] →	Left to Right	Highest Precedence
+ + --	Left to Right	↑
* → *	Left to Right	
* / %	Left to Right	
+ −	Left to Right	
<< >>	Left to Right	
<< = >> =	Left to Right	
= = ! =	Left to Right	
&	Left to Right	
|	Left to Right	
&&	Left to Right	
| |	Left to Right	
? :	Right to Left	
= * = / = % =	Right to Left	
+ = − = & = ∧ =	Right to Left	
| = << = >> =	Right to Left	Lower Precedence

EXPRESSIONS

An expression is any statement which is composed of one or more operands and returns a value. It may be combination of operators, variables and constants.

The expression may be simple to complex.

For example

$a = m + n$; is an expression which adds two variables m and n.

Types of Expressions

1. Constant Expressions
2. Integral Expressions
3. Logical Expressions

Constant Expressions: Constant expressions contain only constant values. The following are constant expressions.

$$12$$
$$12 * 6 + 12/2.0$$

Integral Expressions: Integral expressions are formed by connecting integer constants using arithmetic operators.

The following are integral expressions:

```
const count = 20;
int i, j, k;
```

(*i*) $-i$ (*ii*) j (*iii*) $i - k$

(*iv*) $i + j - k$ (*v*) $j + k$ (*vi*) i/j

(*vii*) $i \% k$ (*viii*) $i * j * k$

Logical Expressions: Logical Expression are those expressions which result in to true or false. These expressions return as 0 or 1 value.

$0 \rightarrow$ false

$1 \rightarrow$ true

The following are the examples of logical expressions

(*i*) $a > b$

(*ii*) $(a + b) > = (a/b)$

(*iii*) $a < = ! b$

TYPE CONVERSION

The process in which one pre-defined type of expressions is converted into another type is called conversion.

There are two types of conversion in C++.

1. Implicit (Automatic) Conversion
2. Explicit Conversion

Implicit Conversion

Data types can be mixed in expressions.

For example

$$a = 6 + 3.5$$

is a valid C++ expression

When data types are mixed in an expression, the conversion is performed automatically. This process of automatic conversion is called implicit conversion.

This conversion is performed without the intervention of the programmer.

Rules for Implicit Conversion

1. If any of the two operands is a long double, the other is converted to a long double.
2. Otherwise, if one of the operands is of type double, the other is converted to double.
3. Otherwise, if one of the operand is float, the other is converted to a float.
4. Otherwise, if one of the operand is unsigned long, the other is converted into unsigned long.
5. Otherwise, if one of the operand is unsigned long, the other is converted into long int.

Explicit Expressions

Explicit expressions are user-defined expressions. C++ provides type casting facility. The expression can be converted into a specific type.

Type casting is done in the following syntax.

(type) expression;

It should be noted that the type casting can be done on the right side of the assignment statement.

Example. Let us have a look on the following program segment.

```
.....................
.....................
int a,b;
double m;
m = a/b;
.....................
.....................
```

The division (/) is removed when the result is performed m is assigned the quotient value. We can also evaluate a/b after converting it to a double expression.

$$m = \text{(double)}\, a/b:$$

ASSIGNMENT STATEMENT

Assignment operator is represented by symbol '='. The Assignment operator takes the value on the right and stores it in the variable on the left side. An expression is composed of one or more operations. An expression itself has a value, which is same value that is assigned to the left hand operand. The assignment operator has right-to-left associativity. Similarly an assignment statement has also right-to-left associativity. Following are some examples of assignment statements.

$a = 12;$

$b = 6.8;$

$c = a + b;$

It must be noted that when we put semicolon after an expression, it becomes a statement.

Operator	Meaning
=	Assignment
– =	Subtract from
+ =	Add to
* =	Multiply by
/=	Divided by
% =	Modulo by
& =	Bitwise AND assignment
^ =	Bitwise XOR assignment
| =	Bitwise OR assignment
<< =	Bitwise shift left assignment
>> =	Bitwise shift right assignment

For example, the expression

sum += *i*; can be written as
sum = sum + *i*;
i = *i* * 6; can be written as
i * = 6;

The main reasons to use arithmetic assignment operator are:

1. Typing work is done easily and can be easily saved.
2. When the variables names are exceptionally long, assignment operators are used to bring simplicity.
3. Spelling mistakes can be avoided.
4. Codes are more readable than lengthy expressions.

VARIABLE INITIALIZATION

In C++, variable is a location to store information. The program can retrieve the value from memory location when required. Any variable in C++ program can be initialized. The process of initialization is performed with the help of assignment statement.

For example

```
int ival=512;
```

The initial value of the integer variable ival is 512.

More than one variable can be initialized at creation.

For example long height=6, width=5;

Here the long variable height is initialized to the value 6 and long variable width to the value 5. We can mix the definition and initialization of the variables as shown below.

```
int xage=15, yage, zage=20;
```

In this example three type int variables have been created. Initialization of the first and third has been done here.

C++ SHORTHANDS

C++ provides shorthands to simplify the coding of a certain type of a assignment statement.

For example

$x = x + 20;$ can be written as

$x + = 20;$

The operator + = instructs the compiler for assigning the value of $x + 20$ to x. General form of C++ shorthand

var=var operator expression

which is same as

var operator=expression

Examples of C++ shorthand

a*=6;	is equivalent to a=a*6;
a/=6;	is equivalent to a=a/6;
a%=b;	is equivalent to a=a%b;

Declaration of Variables

In order to use a variable in C++, we must first declare it specifying which data type we want it to be. The syntax to declare a new variable is to write the specifier of the desired data type (like int, bool, float...) followed by a valid variable identifier. For example:

```
int a;
float mynumber;
```

These are two valid declarations of variables. The first one declares a variable of type `int` with the identifier `a`. The second one declares a variable of type `float` with the identifier `mynumber`. Once declared, the variables a and `mynumber` can be used within the rest of their scope in the program.

If you are going to declare more than one variable of the same type, you can declare all of them in a single statement by separating their identifiers with commas. For example:

```
int a, b, c;
```

This declares three variables (`a`, `b` and `c`), all of them of type `int`, and has exactly the same meaning as:

```
int a;
int b;
int c;
```

The integer data types `char`, `short`, `long` and `int` can be either signed or unsigned depending on the range of numbers needed to be represented. Signed types can represent both positive and negative values, whereas unsigned types can only represent positive values (and zero). This can be specified by using either the specifier `signed` or the specifier `unsigned` before the type name. For example:

```
unsigned short int NumberofTeams;
signed int AccountBalance;
```

By default, if we do not specify either `signed` or `unsigned` most compiler settings will assume the type to be signed, therefore instead of the second declaration above we could have written:

```
int AccountBalance;
```

with exactly the same meaning (with or without the keyword `signed`)

An exception to this general rule is the `char` type, which exists by itself and is considered a different fundamental data type from `signed char` and `unsigned char`, thought to store characters. You should use either `signed` or `unsigned` if you intend to store numerical values in a `char`-sized variable.

`short` and `long` can be used alone as type specifiers. In this case, they refer to their respective integer fundamental types: `short` is equivalent to `short int` and `long` is equivalent to `long int`. The following two variable declarations are equivalent:

```
short Year;
short int Year;
```

Finally, `signed` and `unsigned` may also be used as standalone type specifiers, meaning the same as `signed int` and `unsigned int` respectively. The following two declarations are equivalent:

```
unsigned NextYear;
unsigned int NextYear;
```

Scope of Variables

All the variables that we use in a program must have been declared with its type specifier before their use in the code.

A variable can be either global or local in scope. A global variable is a variable declared in the main body of the source code, outside all functions, while a local variable is one declared within the body of a function or a block.

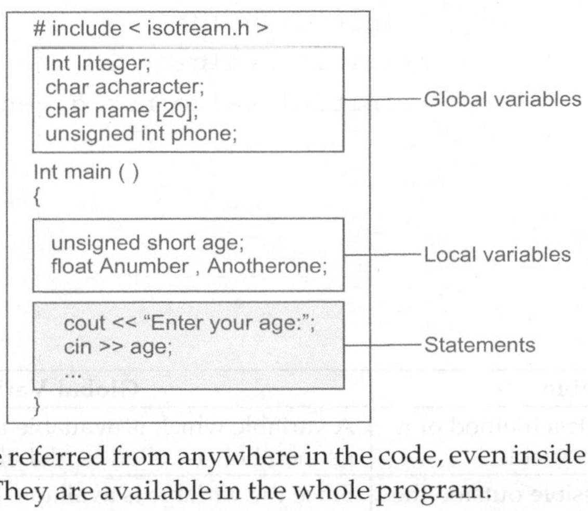

Global variables can be referred from anywhere in the code, even inside functions, whenever they are after its declaration. They are available in the whole program.

The scope of local variables is limited to the block enclosed in braces ({ }) where they are declared. For example, if they are declared at the beginning of the body of a function (like in function `main`) their scope is between its declaration point and the end of that function.

Initialization of Variables

When declaring a regular local variable, its value is by default undetermined. To give it a value, you can initialize the variable. There are two ways to do this in C++:

The first one, is done by appending an equal sign followed by the value to which the variable will be initialized:

```
type identifier = initial_value;
```

For example, if we want to declare an int variable initialized with a value of 0 at the moment in which it is declared, we can write it as -

```
int a = 0;
```

The other way to initialize variables, known as constructor initialization, is done by enclosing the initial value between parentheses (()):

```
type identifier (initial_value);
```

For example:

```
int a (0);
```

Both ways of initializing variables are valid and equivalent in C++.

Example

```
// initialization of variables

#include <iostream.h>

main()
{
    int a=5;                //initial value = 5
    int b(2);               //initial value = 2
    int result;             //initial value not given.

    a = a + 3;
    result = a - b;
    cout<<result;

    return 0;
}
```

Local Variable	Global Variable
A variable declared inside a method or a block is called as a local variable.	A variable which is available to the entire class and its members is called as global variable.
This variable is not accessible outside the method or block in which it is declared.	Since the variable is available globally, any method or block inside the class can access this variable.

Introduction to Strings

Variables that can store non-numerical values and are longer than one single character are known as strings. These non-numerical values are placed in double quotes.

C++ provides support for strings through the standard `string` class. This is not a fundamental type, but it behaves in a similar way as fundamental types do in its most basic usage.

Library file `string.h` is to be included for string handling.

```
//my first string
#include <iostream.h>
#include <string.h>
main()
{
  string mystring = "This is a string";
  cout<<mystring;
  return 0;
}
```

Strings can be initialized with any valid string literal just like numerical type variables can be initialized to any valid numerical literal. Both the following initialization formats are valid.

```
  string mystring = "This is a string";
  string mystring ("This is a string");
```

Strings can also perform all the other basic operations that fundamental data types can, like being declared without an initial value and being assigned values during execution:

```
//my first string
#include<iostream.h>
#include<string.h>

main()
{
  string mystring;
  mystring = "My Example String";
  cout<<mystring<<endl;
  return 0;
}
```

Example. *Write a program which multiplies two variables with postfix incremental operators.*

Solution.

```
//This program obtains the value of multiplication of two
//variables with postfix incremental operators.
#include<iostream.h>
main()
{
      int product;
      int x=20;
      int y=9;
      cout<<"\The value of product is:"<<product;
```

```
        product=(x++)*(y++);          //postfix incremental operators
        cout<<"The product is="<<product;
        return 0;
    }
```

The output of the program will be 180.

Preprocessor Directives

The preprocessor directives are lines included in the programs that are not program statements but directives for the preprocessor. These lines are preceded by a `# sign`. The preprocessor executes before the actual compilation of code begins, therefore the preprocessor takes all these directives before any code is generated by the statements.

These preprocessor directives extend only across a single line of code. As soon as a newline character is found, the preprocessor directive is considered to end. No semicolon (`;`) is placed at the end of a preprocessor directive.

Macro Definitions (#define, #undef)

To define preprocessor macros we can use `#define`. Its format is:

```
#define identifier newitem
```

When the preprocessor encounters this directive, it replaces any occurrence of `identifier` in the rest of the code by `newitem`. This `newitem` can be an expression, a statement, a block or simply anything. The preprocessor does not understand C++, it simply replaces any occurrence of `identifier` by `newitem`.

```
#define TABLE_SIZE 200
int table1[TABLE_SIZE];
int table2[TABLE_SIZE];
```

After the preprocessor has replaced `TABLE_SIZE`, the code becomes equivalent to:

```
int table1[200];
int table2[200];
```

The `#define` can work also with parameters to define function macros:

```
#define getmax(a,b) a>b?a:b
```

This would replace any occurrence of `getmax` followed by two arguments by the replacement expression, but also replacing each argument by its identifier, exactly as you would expect if it was a function:

```
//function macro
#include<iostream.h>
#define getmax (a, b) ((a)>(b)?(a):(b))
int main()
{
  int x=6, y;
  y=getmax(x, 2);
```

```
  cout<<y<< endl;
  cout<<getmax(8, x)<<endl;
  return 0;
}
```

Defined macros are not affected by block structure. A macro lasts until it is undefined with the #undef preprocessor directive:

```
#define TABLE_SIZE 50
int table1[TABLE_SIZE];
#undef TABLE_SIZE
#define TABLE_SIZE 100
int table2[TABLE_SIZE];
```

This would generate the same code as:

```
int table1[50];
int table2[100];
```

Conditional Inclusions (#ifdef, #ifndef, #if, #endif, #else and #elif)

These directive allow to include or discard part of the code of a program if a certain condition is met.

(*i*) `#ifdef` allows a section of a program to be compiled only if the macro that is specified as the parameter has been defined, irrespective of its value. For example:

```
#ifdef TABLE_SIZE
int table[TABLE_SIZE];
#endif
```

In this case, the line of code `int table [TABLE_SIZE];` is only compiled if `TABLE_SIZE` was previously defined with `#define`, independently of its value. If it was not defined, that line will not be included in the program compilation.

(*ii*) `#ifndef` serves for the exact opposite: the code between #ifndef and #endif directives is only compiled if the specified identifier has not been previously defined. For example:

```
#ifndef TABLE_SIZE
#define TABLE_SIZE 50
#endif
int table[TABLE_SIZE];
```

In this case, if when arriving at this piece of code, the TABLE_SIZE macro has not been defined yet, it would be defined to a value of 50. If it already existed it would keep its previous value since the #define directive would not be executed.

(iii) The `#if`, `#else` and `#elif` directives serve to specify some condition to be met in order for the portion of code they surround to be compiled. The condition that follows `#if` or `#elif` can only evaluate constant expressions, including macro expressions. For example:

```
#if TABLE_SIZE>200
#undef TABLE_SIZE
#define TABLE_SIZE 200
```

```
#elif TABLE_SIZE<50
#undef TABLE_SIZE
#define TABLE_SIZE 50
#else
#undef TABLE_SIZE
#define TABLE_SIZE 100
#endif
int table[TABLE_SIZE];
```

Notice how the whole structure of `#if`, `#elif` and `#else` chained directives ends with `#endif`.

The behavior of `#ifdef` and `#ifndef` can also be achieved by using the special operators `defined` and `!defined` respectively in any `#if` or `#elif` directive:

```
#if !defined TABLE_SIZE
#define TABLE_SIZE 100
#elif defined ARRAY_SIZE
#define TABLE_SIZE ARRAY_SIZE
int table [TABLE_SIZE];
```

Line Control (#line)

When we compile a program and some error happen during the compiling process, the compiler shows an error message with references to the name of the file where the error happened and a line number, so it is easier to find the code generating the error.

The `#line` directive allows us to control both things, the line numbers within the code files as well as the file name that we want that appears when an error takes place. Its format is:

```
#line number "filename"
```

Where `number` is the new line number that will be assigned to the next code line. The line numbers of successive lines will be increased one by one from this point on.

`"filename"` is an optional parameter that allows to redefine the file name that will be shown. For example:

```
#line 20 "assigning variable"
int a ?;
```

This code will generate an error that will be shown as error in file `"assigning variable"`, line 20.

Error Directive (#error)

This directive aborts the compilation process when it is found, generating a compilation the error that can be specified as its parameter:

```
#ifndef_cplusplus
#error AC++ compiler is required!
#endif
```

This example aborts the compilation process if the macro name `_cplusplus` is not defined(this macro name is defined by default in all C++ compilers).

Source File Inclusion (#include)

This directive has also been used frequently in other sections of this book. When the preprocessor finds an `#include` directive it replaces it by the entire content of the specified file. There are two ways to specify a file to be included:

```
#include "file"
#include <file>
```

The only difference between both expressions is the places (directories) where the compiler is going to look for the file. In the first case where the file name is specified between double-quotes, the file is searched first in the same directory that includes the file containing the directive. In case that it is not there, the compiler searches the file in the default directories where it is configured to look for the standard header files.

If the file name is enclosed between angle-brackets <> the file is searched directly where the compiler is configured to look for the standard header files. Therefore, standard header files are usually included in angle-brackets, while other specific header files are included using double quotes.

4

DECISION-MAKING AND FLOW OF CONTROL

COMPOUND STATEMENT

A compound statement is a grouping of statements in which each individual statement ends with a semi-colon. The group of statements is also called **Block**. Compound statement is enclosed between the pair of braces ({ }). The opening brace ({) signifies the beginning and closing brace (}) signifies the end of the block.

Example

```
{
  cin>>length >>breadth;
  perimeter=2*(length+breadth);
  cout<<"perimeter"<<perimeter;
}
```

Conditional Statements

Sometimes the program is to be executed depending upon a particular condition. 'If' statement is used for this selective execution (conditional statements).

'If' Statement

The 'if' statement helps in selecting one alternative out of the two. The execution of 'if' statement starts with the evaluation of the condition. The 'if' statement, therefore, helps the programmer to test for the condition.

General Form of 'if' statement

```
if (expression)
statement;
```

Any expression can appear in the parentheses of the 'if'statement. If the expression has 0 (zero) value, it is considered as false. If the value is non-zero, this is true. C++ provides the following constructs for implementing the selection control structure.

–If-construct

–If-else construct

–If-else-if construct

–If-If-else construct

–Switch construct

Flow Chart of If-Construct

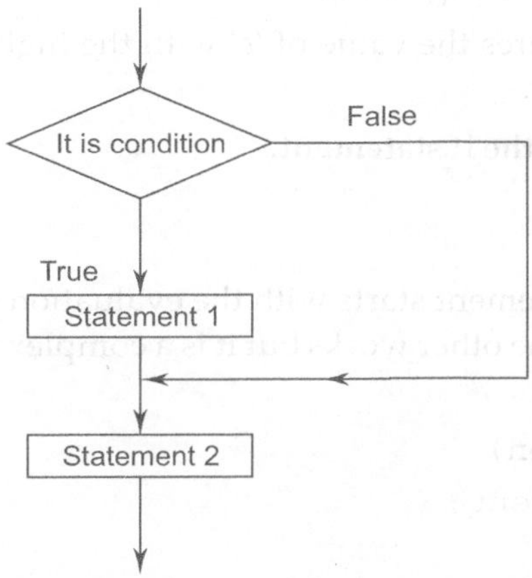

From the chart it is clear that if the condition is True, Statement 1 is executed and then Statement 2 is executed. If the condition is False, Statement 1 is not executed and directly Statement 2 is executed.

Illustration: *Develop a C++ program to find the greatest number out of the three +ve numbers using **if** construct.*

Solution:

```
//This program finds the greatest of the three numbers
#include <iostream.h>
main()
{
  int a, b, c, greatest; //a, b, c, are given numbers
  cin>>a>>b>>c>>;        //input a, b, c
  greatest=a;            //greatest is assigned the value
  if(b>greatest)
  greatest=b;
  if(c>greatest)
  greatest=c;
  cout<<"\The greatest number="<<greatest;
  return 0;
}
```

Explanation

In this C++ program, the greatest identifier is assigned the value of '*a*'. The value of '*b*' is compared with that of greatest. If *b*>greatest,

the statement

greatest = *b*; is executed

If *b* < greatest, the statement

greatest = *b*; is ignored.

Now the 'if' statement compares the value of '*c*' with the highest number. If *c*> greatest, then greatest is assigned the value of *c*.

A semicolon must not follow the if statement.

If-else Construct

The execution of the 'if-else' statement starts with the evaluation of the condition. The method of testing one condition and then the other works but it is a complex one. The keyword else provides readable code.

```
if(expression)
        statement;
else
        statement;
```

Flow Chart of If-Else Statement

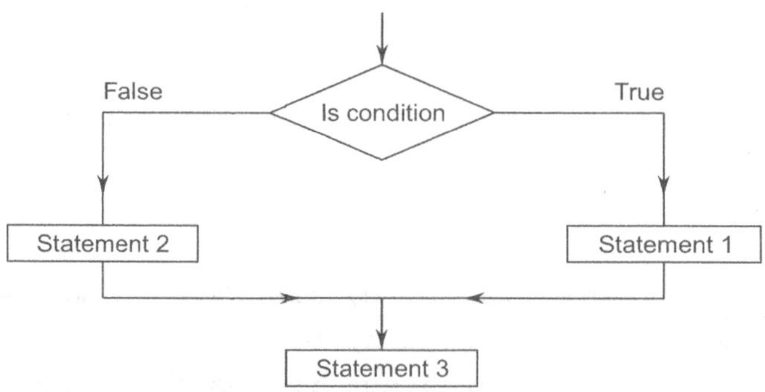

If the condition is True, Statement 1 is executed followed by Statement 3. Statement 2 is not executed. If the condition is False, Statement 2 is followed by Statement 3. In this case Statement 1 is not executed.

Illustration: *Develop a C++ program to find the value of the following expression, where a, b, c, are constants and belong to the data type float.*

$$y = ax^2 + bx + c; \text{if } x >= 4$$
$$= -ax^2 + bx - c; \text{if } x < 4$$

Solution:

```
//This program evaluates an expression
#include<iostream.h>
#include<math.h>

main()
{
 float a,b,c,x,y;
 cin>>a>>b>>c>>x;          //value of constant and other parameters
 if(x>=4)
  y=a*x*x + b*x + c;
 else
  y = - a*x*x + b*x - c;
 cout<<"The value of y="<<y;
 return();
}
```

If-else-If Construct

The if-else-if construct can be shown as below:

```
if(condition 1)
   Statement 1
else
if(condition 2)
   Statement 2
else
if(condition n)
   Statement n
```

Execution of if-else Construct

First the condition 1 is tested and if it is true then, Statement 1 is executed and all other if-else-if construct end.

If condition 1 is false, then the statement is ignored and condition 2 is tested. If it is True then Statement 2 is executed and remaining if-else-if construct is terminated and if the condition 2 is False, Statement 2 is ignored and condition 3 is tested. This process continues in this way.

Illustration 1. *To foster a sense of water conservation, the water department has an annual water conservation tax policy. The rates are based on the water consumption of the consumer. The tax rules are as follows:*

Sales	Commission
More than 45 but 75 or less	475.00
More than 75 but 125 or less	750.00
More than 125 but 200 or less	1225.00
More than 200 but 350 or less	1650.00
More than 350	2000.00

Write a program in C++ to compute and display an annual water tax based on the input of water consumption.

Program in C++

```
#include<iostream.h>
main()
{
  int units;
  float charges;
  charges=0;
  cout<<"\n Enter Units Consumed=";
  cin>>units;
  if(units>45||units<75)
  charges=475.00;
  else if(units>75||units<125)
  charges= 750.00;
  else if(units>125||units<200)
  charges=1225.00;
  else if(units>200||units<350)
  charges=1650.00;
  else
  charges=2000.00;
  cout<<"\n units="<<units;
  cout<<"n charges="<<charges;
}
```

Nested If Statement

The statement sequence of if or else can consist another if statement, *i.e.*, the if-else statements can be nested in one another.

```
Execution of nested   if statement
                      if(exp1)
                      if(exp2)
```

```
        {
        ..............................
        ..............................
        ..............................
        }
else
    if(exp3)
        {
        ..............................
        ..............................
        ..............................
else
        ..............................
        ..............................
        ..............................
}
```

Switch Statement

Switch construct is a powerful construct provided in C++. If one of several courses of action is to be selected, switch statement can be used.

The syntax of switch statement is as follows:

```
switch(expression)
{
  case constant1
     statement sequence1;
  case constant2
     statement sequence2;
..................................
..................................
```

The purpose of switch statement is to select one of many possible statements to execute.

The `if` statement allows you to select one of two sections of code to execute based on a Boolean value (only two possible values). The `switch` statement allows you to choose from many statements based on an integer (including `char`) or enum value.

The `switch` keyword is followed by a parenthesized integer expression, which is followed by the *cases*, all enclosed in braces. The switch statement executes the case corresponding to the value of the expression. Normally the code in a case clause ends with a `break` statement, which exits the switch statement and continues with the statement following the switch. If there is no corresponding case value, the `default` clause is executed. If no case matched and there is no default clause, execution continues after the end of the switch statement.

The case keyword is followed by an integer constant and a colon. This begins the statements that are executed when the switch expression has that case value.

Switch Statement	If Statement
The purpose of switch statement is to select one of many possible statements to execute.	It is a decision-making branching statement. Tells the computer to take one of two alternative courses of action.
The switch statement allows you to choose from many statements based on an integer (including char) or enum value.	The if statement allows you to select one of two sections of code to execute base on a Boolean value (only two possible values true or false.)

Execution of Switch Statement

The execution of switch statement begins with the evaluation of expression. If the expression evaluates to constant the execution of switch starts with the statement with constant n. All other statements following this statement execute sequentially.

If the value of expression does not reconcile with the constant1, constant2,... the statement with default is executed.

Flow Chart for Switch Statement

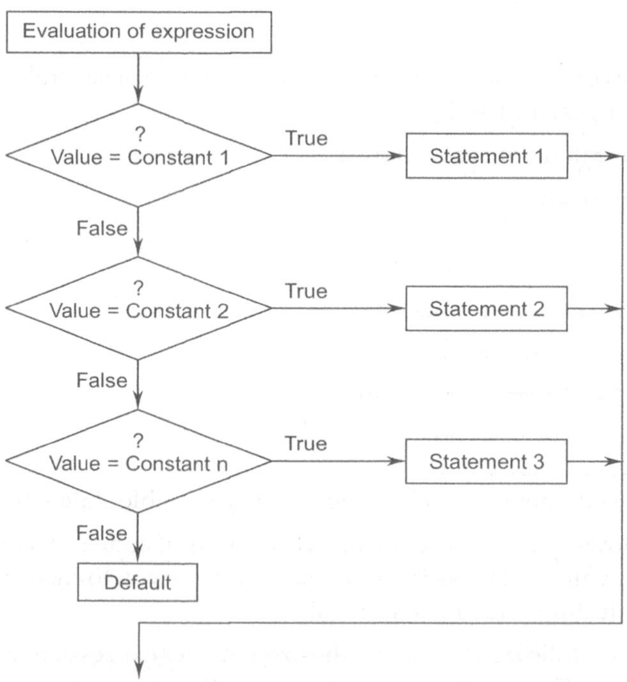

Execution of Switch Statement with Break Statement

The break statement following a particular statement series brings the termination of the **Switch Construct** and skips over the remaining statement series without execution.

No semicolon is allowed with Switch construct. Case Statements should be integers or characters. No number with a decimal point should be there (with case statement).

Illustration: *M/s Firewall Publishers, the pioneer publishers of textbooks, allow the different discounts on different types of textbooks, as below.*

1. *Mathematics books* — *discount 15% if the order is Rs. 5000/- or more.*
2. *Computer books* — *discount 25% if the value of the order is Rs. 6,000/- or more.*
3. *Question Bank* — *discount 30% if the value of the order is Rs. 3000/- or more.*
4. *Hindi Books* — *discount 30% if the value of order is Rs. 1000 or more.*

Develop a C++ program for the above data and determine the net amount payable.

Solution:

```
//This program determines the discount
//and the net amount using switch statement
#include<iostream.h>
#include<math.h>
main()
{
  int books;
  float order_amount disc, net_amount;
      cin>>books;
      cin>>order_amount;
  switch(code)
  {
  case 1: if(order_amount>=5000)
  disc=0.15;
  else
  disc=0;
  break;
  case 2: if(order_amount>=6000)
  disc=0.25;
  else
  disc=0;
  break;
  case 3: if(order_amount>=3000)
  disc=0.30;
  else
  disc=0;
  break;
  case 4: if(order_amount>=1000)
  disc=0.30;
```

```
    else
    disc=0;
    }
    net_amount=order_amount*(1-disc);
    cout<<"net_amount="<net_amount;
    return 0;
}
```

In this program case 4 does not have **break**. If case 4 is **executed** the switch construct would terminate.

Equivalence of Switch Statement with If Statement

A `switch` statement can often be rewritten as an `if` statement in a straightforward manner. For example, the preceding `switch` statement could be written as follows. When one of a number of blocks of code is selected based on a single value, the `switch` statement is generally easier to read. The choice of `if` or `switch` should be based on which is more readable.

Conditions when Use of Switch Statement is Viable

The ability of `switch` to choose between many sections of code seems to make it more powerful than `if`. However, selecting sections of code depending on specific integer values turns out not to be very common. If you are handling specific coded values or processing characters (whose codes are treated like numbers), you may find it useful.

Some compilers can produce more efficient code for certain `switch` statements than for equivalent `if` statements. I have't bothered to test the C++ compiler because, if there is a speed difference, it would be extremely small and the choice between `switch` and `if` should be based on readability.

COMMA OPERATOR

Generally a comma operator is used to form a compound expression. A comma operator (,) allows the user to push through two C++ arithmetic expressions.

General Syntax	(expression_1, expression_2)

These two expressions are counted as a single expression.

Example

```
(a, b)              //two expression a, b count as a
                    //single expression.
(a=30, 2*b+30)      //Value of expression is 90, the
                    //Value of 2nd expression
```

Sometimes comma does not represent as a comma operator and instead serves as a separator only.

```
int a,b;
```

Here (,) is a separator.

In a for loop in C++, comma operator separates the initialization expression.

for (i=0, j=10; i<=10; i++, j--)

Here the initialization expressions have been separated by comma.

Break Statement	Continue Statement
The break statement is used when you want to skip over a loop instead of exiting the entire program.	The continue statement does opposite of the break statement.
This statement is used with while, do while, for or switch statements.	It forces the next iteration of the loop. The computer ignores any other statement in the loop that follows the continue statement.

EXIT FUNCTION

The `exit()` function helps in terminating the program. It terminates as a break statement.

General Syntax	`exit(n);`

where n is any argument either 0 or 1.

When the `exit()` function is carried, the program terminates in normal way. If we use exit (1), the program terminates abnormally and with (0) it terminates normally.

Example

```
main()
{
      :
      :
      if (root_1<=0)
      exit();
      :
      :
}
```

The following program shows the use of exit() function

```
//use of exit()
#include<iostream.h>
#include<process.h>
int main()
{
   int number, x;
   cout<<"Enter Number=";
   cin>>number;
   for(x=2; x<=number/7; ++x)
   if(number%x==0)
   {
      cout<<"Number Divisible by" 7;
```

```
        exit(0);
    }
    cout<<"Number not Divisible by 7";
}
```

Output of the Program

Enter Number = 777

Number Divisible by 7

Another Run

Enter Number = 521

Number not Divisible by 7.

LOOP CONSTRUCT

Loop construct is also Repetitive Control Structure in nature. Sometimes we require a set of statements to be executed number of times by changing the values of one or more variables each time to obtain a different result. This type of program execution is called looping. C++ provides the following loop constructs.

1. while loop
2. do while Loop
3. for Loop

While Loop

The while loop construct is used for repetitive executive of a program subject to the conditions which may have Zero (False) or Non-Zero (True) value.

General Syntax for the while loop.

```
while (condition) statement;
```

while is a keyword of C++, condition is an expression and the statement can be a simple or compound one.

Flow Chart for the While Loop

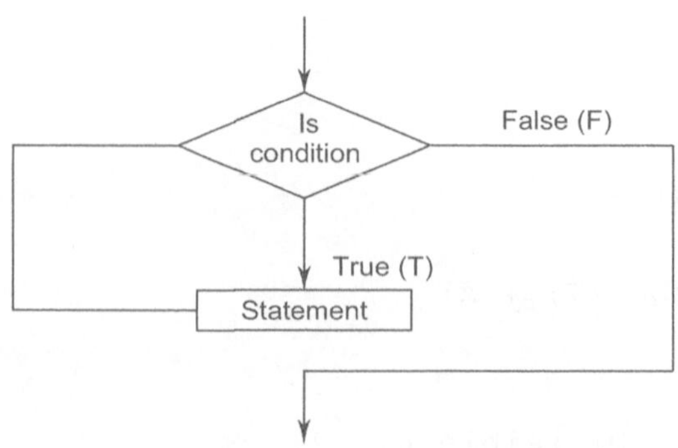

In the flow chart of the condition evaluates to a non-zero(true) execution, the condition is evaluated again and if the condition evaluates to a zero (false) execution, the while loop is terminated.

Illustration 1: *Write a C++ program which calculates the average and sum of numbers using while loop.*

Solution:

```
//This program calculates the average and sum of the given
//numbers using while loop
#include<iostream.h>
#include<math.h>
main()
{
  int number, i;
  float average;
  float sum;
  float x;
  cout<<"\n How many numbers you want to enter?"
  cin>>number;
  sum=0;
  i=0;
  while(i<=number-1)
  {
    cout<<"Enter Number";
    cin>>x;
    sum=sum+x;
    ++i;
  }
  average=sum/number;
  cout<<"Sum of These Numbers is = "<<sum;
  cout<<"Average of the Numbers is = "<<average<<endl;
  }
```

Run of the Program

How many numbers you want to Enter? 5

1

2

3

4

5

Sum of These Numbers is = 15

Average of the Numbers is = 3

The Do While Loop

Like a while loop, the do while loop is another repetitive control structure. In while loop the condition is tested before execution whereas in a do while loop the condition is tested after execution.

General Syntax —

```
do
  {
       statement;
  }
while(condition);
```

Condition may be a single or compound statement. The condition may have 0 or non-zero.

do while	while
1. The loop executes the statement at least once.	1. The statements can be executed.
2. The condition is tested after execution.	2. The condition is tested before execution.
3. If the condition is false, the computer keeps executing the loop.	3. The loop laminates if the condition becomes false.

Illustration 1: *Write a program in C++ which calculates the average and sum of the given numbers using do while loop.*

Solution:

```
//This program calculates the average and sum of the given
//numbers using do while loop
#include<iostream.h>
#include<math.h>
main()
{
   int number, i;
   float average;
   float sum;
   float x;
   cout<<"\n How many numbers you want to enter?";
   cin>>number;
   sum=0;
   i=0;
   do
   {
```

```
        cout<<"\n Enter Number";
        cin>>x;
        sum=sum+x;
        i++;
    }
    while(i<=number-1);
    average=sum/number;
    cout<<"\n Sum of These Numbers is="<<sum<<endl;
    cout<<"\n Average of the Numbers is="<<average;
}
```

Run of the Program

How many numbers you want to Enter? 5

1

2

3

4

5

Sum of These Numbers is = 15

Average of the Numbers is = 3

The For Loop

The for loop is also used for repetitive execution of C++ program but for a mixed number of times. The program knows well in advance how many times the loop is to be executed.

General Syntax—

```
for (initial expression; test expression;update expression)
   {
      statement;
   }
```

This loop is executed at initial value, middle value and final value.

Execution of a For Loop

1. In first step, the initial expression is evaluated.
2. In next step, the test-expression is evaluated.
   If the value is non-zero, the loop is executed.
   and if the value is zero, the loop is terminated without execution.
3. After the execution of for loop, the update expression is evaluated.

Flow Chart for Execution of For Loop

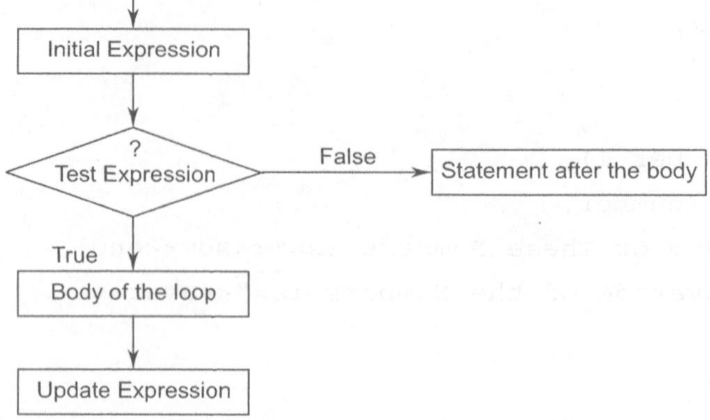

Illustration 1: *What will be the output of the following program?*

```
#include<iostream.h>
main()
{
  int a;
  for(a=0;a<=20;++a)
  {
    cout<<a;
  }
}
```

Solution:

Output of the program

0 1 2 3 4 5 6 7 8 9 10 11 12 13 14 15 16 17 18 19 20

Illustration 2: *Write a program to find the square of first 20 numbers using for loop.*

Solution:

```
//This program demonstrates the use of for loop.
#include<iostream.h>
main()
{
  int a;
  for(a=0;a<=20;++a)
  cout<<a*a" ";
}
```

Output of the program

0 1 4 9 16 25 36 49 64 81 100 121 144 169 196 225 256 289 324 361 400

SOME MORE WORKED-OUT EXAMPLES

1. Write a program that reads the sides of a triangle and determines whether a right angle triangle can be formed with the given data.

Solution:

```
//This program finds whether a right angle triangle can be
//formed using the sides of a triangle
#include<iostream.h>
main()
{
  int a, b, c;                          //Three sides of a triangle.
    cout<<"\n Enter three sides";
    cin>>a;
    cin>>b;
    cin>>c;
  if(a*a+b*b==c*c)
  cout<<"The right angle triangle exists";
  else
  cout<<\"The right angle triangle does not exist";
}
```

2. Write a C++ program which calculates the larger number out of the two.

Solution:

```
//This program calculates the larger number out of the two.
#include<iostream.h>
main()
{
  double num1,num2;
  cout<<"\n Enter two numbers";
  cin>>num1>>num2;
  if(num1>num2)
  cout<<"Number1 is the bigger number";
  cout<<"\n The bigger number is:"<<num1;
    else
    cout<<"Number2 is the bigger number";
    cout<<"The bigger number is:"<<num2;
  return 0;
}
```

3. Write a C++ program to calculate the sum and average of the given numbers. (Use do while loop).

Solution:

```
//This program calculates the sum and average of the given numbers
#include<iostream.h>
#include<math.h>
void main(void)
{
    int i, n;
    float average, x, sum;
    cout<<"\How many Numbers:";
    cin>>n;
    i=0;
    sum=0;
    do
    {
     cout<<"Enter a Number";
     cin>>x;
     sum=sum+x;
     i++;
    }
    while(i<=n-1);
    average=sum/n;
    cout<<"\n The sum of given Numbers is"<<sum;
    cout<<"\n Average is:"<<average;
}
```

Exceptions

Exceptions provide a way to react to exceptional circumstances (like runtime errors) in our program by transferring control to special functions called *handlers*.

To catch exceptions we have to place a portion of code under exception inspection. This is done by enclosing that portion of code in a *try block*. When an exceptional situation arises within that block, an exception is thrown. This exception transfers the control to the exception handler. If no exception is thrown, the code continues normally and all handlers are ignored.

An exception is thrown by using the throw keyword from inside the try block. Exception handlers are declared with the keyword `catch`, which must be placed immediately after the try block:

```
//exceptions
#include<iostream.h>

main() {
  try
  {
    throw 30;
```

```
    }
    catch(int e)
    {
      cout<<"An exception occurred. "<<e<< endl;
    }
    return 0;
}
```

The code under exception handling is enclosed in a `try` block. In this example this code simply throws an exception:

```
throw 30;
```

A throw expression accepts one parameter (here integer value `30`), which is passed as an argument to the exception handler.

The exception handler is declared with the `catch` keyword. It follows immediately the closing brace of the `try` block. The catch format is similar to a regular function that always has at least one parameter. The type of this parameter is very important, since the type of the argument passed by the throw expression is checked against it and only in the case they match, the exception is caught.

We can chain multiple handlers (catch expressions), each one with a different parameter type. Only the handler that matches its type with the argument specified in the throw statement is executed.

It is also possible to nest `try-catch` blocks within more external `try` blocks. In these cases, we have the possibility that an internal `catch` block forwards the exception to its external level. This is done with the expression `throw;` with no arguments. For example:

```
try {
  try {
      //code here
  }
  catch(int n) {
      throw;
  }
}
catch(...){
  cout<<"Exception occurred";
}
```

Exception Specifications

When we declare a function we can limit the exception type it might directly or indirectly throw by appending a `throw` suffix to the function declaration:

```
float myfunction (char param) throw (int);
```

This declares a function called `myfunction` which takes one argument of type `char` and returns an element of type `float`. The only exception that this function might throw is an exception of type int. If it throws an exception with a different type, either directly or indirectly, it cannot be caught by a regular int-type handler.

If this throw specifier is left empty with no type, this means the function is not allowed to throw exceptions. Functions with no throw specifier (regular functions) are allowed to throw exceptions with any type:

```
int myfunction (int param) throw();   //no exceptions allowed
int myfunction (int param);           //all exceptions allowed
```

Standard Exceptions

The C++ Standard library provides a base class specifically designed to declare objects to be thrown as exceptions. It is called exception and is defined in the <exception> header file under the namespace std. This class has the usual default and copy constructors, operators and destructors, plus an additional virtual member function called what that returns a null-terminated character sequence(char *) and that can be overwritten in derived classes to contain some sort of description of the exception.

```
//standard exceptions
#include<iostream.h>
#include<exception.h>
class myexception: public exception
{
  virtual const char* what() const throw()
  {
    return"My exception happened";
  }
} myex;

int main() {
  try
  {
    throw myex;
  }
  catch(exception &e)
  {
    cout<<e.what()<<endl;
  }
  return 0;
}
```

We have placed a handler that catches exception objects by reference (notice the ampersand & after the type), therefore this catches also classes derived from exception, like our myex object of class myexception.

All exceptions thrown by components of the C++ Standard library throw exceptions derived from this std:: exception class. These are:

Exception	Description
bad_alloc	is thrown by new on allocation failure
bad_cast	is thrown by dynamic_cast when fails with a referenced type
bad_exception	is thrown when an exception type doesn't match any catch
bad_typeid	is thrown by typeid
ios_base::failure	is thrown by functions in the iostream library

For example, if we use the operator new and the memory cannot be allocated, an exception of type `bad_alloc` is thrown:

```
try
{
   int *myarray=new int[500];
}
   catch(bad_alloc&)
{
   cout<<"Error allocating memory."<<endl;
}
```

It is recommended to include all dynamic memory allocations within a try block that catches this type of exception to perform a clean action instead of an abnormal program termination, which is what happens when this type of exception is thrown and not caught. If you want to force a `bad_alloc` exception to see it in action, you can try to allocate a huge array; On my system, trying to allocate 1 billion `ints` threw a `bad_alloc` exception.

Because `bad_alloc` is derived from the standard base class `exception`, we can handle that same exception by catching references to the `exception` class:

```
//bad_alloc standard exception
#include<iostream.h>
#include<exception.h>

int main() {
  try
  {
    int*myarray=new int[500];
  }
  catch(exception &e)
  {
    cout<<"Standard exception:" <<e.what()<<endl;
  }
  return 0;
}
main()
{
```

```
    int base, height;
    cout<<"Enter Base of the triangle =";
    cin>>base;
    cout<<"Enter Height of the triangle =";
    cin>>height
    cout<<"The Hypotenuse of the triangle is="<<hypot(base, height);
}
```

Ouptut of the Program

Enter Base=8

Enter Height=6

The Hypotenuse is =10

5

CONSOLE I/O FUNCTIONS

INTRODUCTION

Input/Output (I/O) functions are not directly performed by C++. These are the header files which help in performing input/output functions. **cin** and **cout** functions help in performing input and output activities. For cin and cout, we have to include iostream.h header file.

```
#include<iostream.h>
```

C++ provides a number of functions to deal with characters and input/output operations.

These functions are:

1. getchar()
2. putchar()
3. gets()
4. puts()

These functions are also termed as unformatted console I/O functions.

In C++ programming the keyboard is a standard input device and a monitor is standard output device.

Standard Devices in C++

Description	C++ Name
Keyboard	stdin
Screen	stdout
Printer	stdprn
Serial Port	stdaux
Error Message	stderr

Character Functions getchar() and putchar()

These functions are based on characters for input and output operations.

getchar(): The function getchar() reads a single character from the standard input device which is usually a keyboard.

It is worth noting when getchar() is used, the execution of the program is temporarily suspended. When the character is typed by the user from the keyboard, then this character is communicated to the program. The suspended execution starts again. No argument (s) is (are) required in the function because getchar() function reads a single character in a given time.

```
........................
........................
char ch;
ch=getchar();
........................
........................
```

The function getchar() is included in stdio.h header file.

putchar(): The putchar() function is used to send a single character on the monitor.

Argument is used in this function. When putchar function is executed, the character related with the argument is displayed on VDU screen.

Syntax of putchar() function.

putchar(c); where *c* is any argument

The function putchar() is also included in stdio.h header file.

Illustration 1: *Write a C++ program which demonstrates the use of putchar () function.*

Solution:

```
//This program illustrates the use of putchar () function.
#include<iostream.h>
#include<stdio.h>
main()
{
  char alphabet;
  for(alphabet='a';alphabet<='z'; alphabet++)
  putchar(alphabet);
}
```

Illustration 2: *Write a small C++ program which illustrates the use of getchar().*

Solution:

```
//This program illustrates the use of getchar () function.
#include<iostream.h>
#include<stdio.h>
main()
{
  char character;
  cout<<"Enter the character:";
```

```
    character=getchar();
    if(character==' ')
    cout<<"It is Blank Space";
    else
    cout<<"It is a character";
}
```

The get() function

The get() function is an input function. The get() function inputs a single character from the standard input device. This is used with cin.

The format of get() function is as under:

```
char chr;
cin.get(chr);
```

The put() function

The put() function is an output function. This function reads a single character and outputs the single character to standard output device.

The put() function is used with cout.

```
char chr;
cout.put(chr);
```

It should be noted that get() and put() cannot be used alone. get() and put() are single character functions.

Illustration 1: *The following program counts the number of characters used in a sentence.*

Solution:

```
#include<iostream.h>
#include<string.h>
#include<stdio.h>
main()
{
  char chr;
  int count=0;
  cout<<"Enter sentence";
  cin.get(chr);
  while(chr!='n')
  {
    count++;
    cout.put(chr);
    cin.get(chr);
```

```
    }
    cout<<"Number of character="<<count<<endl;
    return 0;
```

Use of cin with get ()

Input stream object cin can be used as cin.get(). The prefix cin in the get() function that this is the member function of the cin object.

Illustration 1: The following program counts the number of '*' used in the tream.

```
#include<iostream.h>
main()
{
char line;
int count=0;
while(cin.get(line))
if(line=='*')
++count;
cout<<"Number of *is";
cout<<count<<endl;
return 0;
}
```

gets() and puts() functions

The function gets() and puts() are string functions which are commonly used to handle character strings. These functions are contained in stdio.h header file.

The gets () function: This function reads a string from the input device, *i.e.*, keyboard.

General Syntax

```
gets(string);
```

This is an unformatted function. As soon as the command of gets() is encountered, the program temporarily halts and restarts as and when the user enters the characters of the string. It is advisable to use **fflush(stdin)** in the program to avoid any interference.

The puts () function: This function puts string or sends string to the output device or to the monitor.

General Syntax—

```
puts(string);
```

String may be any argument. Once the program is executed, message is displayed on the monitor.

Illustration 1: *Develop a C++ program which illustrates the use of gets() and puts() functions.*

Solution:

```
//This program illustrates the use of gets() and puts() functions.
```

```
#include<iostream.h>
#include<stdio.h>
main()
{
      char name[];
      puts("Enter publisher name") //reads the size of string
      name=getchar();
      fflush(stdin);               //clears input buffer
      puts(name);
      return 0;
}
```

Multicharacter Functions

The getline() function: The getline() function is almost similar to the get() function.

The getline() function is an input function. It reads a line of text which ends with a newline character.

The format of getline() function is

```
cin.getline(line, size);
```

where line is the name of variable which stores the line of text and size specifies the maximum number of characters which can be stored in line.

Examples

```
char name[40];
cin.getline(name, 40);
```

The function getline() can also read white spaces (blank space, tabs etc.) and newline characters.

Illustration 1:

```
#include<iostream.h>
main()
{
      char name[40];
      cout<<"Enter name";
      cin.getline(name, 40);
      cout<<name;
      return;
}
```

The write () function: The write() function is an output function and this can display entire line of text. The format of write() function is

```
cout.write(line, size);
```

Here, line specifies the string variable whose contents are to be displayed and size specifies the maximum number of characters to be displayed.

```
char [40];
cout.write(name, 40);
```

It is also possible to combine two write() functions as shown below

```
cout.write(S1, size1),write(S2, size2);
```

where S1 and S2 are two strings. The above statement prints string S1 and string S2 in the same line.

6

STANDARD LIBRARY FUNCTIONS AND HEADER FILES

LIBRARIES

A library is a collection of linkable files or programs or functions that can be used by the other programs. Library functions are predefined functions provided by C++. These functions are very useful for the programmer because a lot of time is saved due to predefinedness of these functions and the programmer need not write the codes of these functions.

Features of Library Functions

1. **Time Saving:** Library functions being pre-defined, save time. The efforts of redevelopment can be avoided.
2. **Fast Process:** Program development is faster.
3. **Sharing:** Library functions can be shared by different users.
4. **Lesser Disk Space:** These functions occupy a lesser space on the disk. Only one copy is to be maintained.

The Standard C++ Libraries

Dozens of libraries are available which provide file manipulation and other functions. It is notable that all the standard functions are included in Header Files. These header files are also known as Library Files. Each function library has a corresponding header file having extension '*h*'. When a standard function is used in a program, the header file with this function must be included in the program by pre-processor directive include.

```
#include<name_of_header_file>
```

It is worth noting that these pre-processor directives should be placed before the main() function.

Various Header Files

1. stdio.h
2. string.h
3. math.h
4. stdlib.h
5. iostream.h
6. iomanip.h
7. ctype.h
8. process.h

9. time.h	10. values.h	11. dir.h	12. stat.h
13. share.h	14. dos.h		

Header File stdio.h

This file is used for the purpose of declaration for standard I/O functions. Some functions in this file are:

1. clearerr	2. fcloseall	3. fdopen	4. fetcher
5. fopen	6. fputs	7. fread	8. fwrite
9. getc	10. printf	11. putc	12. putchar
13. puts	14. remove	15. rename	16. scanf
17. setupf	18. sprintf	19. vfscanf	20. vprintf

Header File string.h

String library is most popular library. Some functions in this file are:

1. memcpy	2. memset	3. strcpy	4. strchr
5. strcoll	6. strcmp	7. strlen	8. strnset
9. strchr	10. strrew	11. strspn	12. strctr
13. strtok	14. strdup	15. strerror	16. strcmpi
17. strxfrm	18. strpbrk	19. strstr	

Purpose of some functions in string.h header file

1. strcpy — This is used to copy a string into another.
   General Syntax—strcpy (string, string2);
2. strchr — This is used to scan a given string for the first occurrence of a character in a string.
   General Syntax—strchr (string,ch);
3. strstr — This is used to locate the position of a substring.
   General Syntax—strstr(string1, string2);

Header File math.h

This file consists of the functions required for the purpose of mathematical operations. Algebraic, trigonometric and other allied functions are solved with this file.

The various functions in this file are given below:

1. abs	2. acos	3. arg	4. asin
5. atan	6. log	7. log10	8. cos
9. exp	10. sin	11. sinh	12. cosh
13. tan	14. tanh	15. sqrt	16. tanl
17. logl	18. logio	19. div	20. floor
21. floorl	22. sqrtl	23. polyl	24. sinl
25. hypot	26. flexpl	27. tanhl	28. hypoll
29. finod	30. fabs	31. coshl	32. poly

The following table contains the various functions used in math.h header file.

S.N.	Functions	Syntax	Purpose
1.	e^x	double exp (double x),	To determine value of e
2.	$\log_{10} x$	double by (double x);	To determine value $\log_{10} x$
3.	$\sqrt{x}$	double sqrt (double x);	To obtain the square root of x
4.	tan (x)	double tan x (double x);	To obtain the value of tan x
5.	cos (x)	double cos x (double x);	To obtain the value of cos x
6.	sin (x)	double sin x (double x);	To obtain the value of sin x
7.	$\cos^{-1} (x)$	double acos (double x);	To obtain the value of $\cos^{-1} x$
8.	$\sin^{-1} (x)$	double asin (double x);	To obtain the value of $\sin^{-1} x$

Header File stdlib.h

The stdlib.h header file consists of a miscellaneous collection of functions. Stdlib library includes simple integers math functions, sorting functions. There is another important thing, *i.e.*, of text-conversions (ASCII to integers).

Various functions used in this file are furnished below:

1. abs	2. abort	3. atof	4. atoi
5. atol	6. exit	7. free	8. labs
9. itoa	10. qsort	11. random	12. strand
13. wctomb	14. strtol	15. fcvt	16. coreleft
17. malloc	18. realloc	19. ecvt	20. ultoa

S.N.	Function	Use/purpose
1.	abs( )	To obtain absolute value of an integer
2.	atoi( )	Integer conversion
3.	qsort( )	To sort a table
4.	Abort( )	To terminate the program without closing files

Header File iostream.h

In previous chapters we have seen that header file iostream.h was used for input and output functions (cin and cout).

General Syntax—

```
#include<iostream.h>
```

Various functions used in iostream.h header file are

1. eof	2. fill	3. fail	4. put
5. read	6. write	7. open	8. close
9. good	10. getline	11. clear	12. bad
13. peek			

Header File iomanip.h

We can format output with the help of manipulators provided by C++.

Some of the manipulators provided by this library are given below:

1. setw
2. endl
3. setprecision
4. setfill
5. dec
6. hex
7. oct
8. ws
9. ends
10. flush

Functions	Syntax	Purpose
setw	setw(n);	an expression
endl	endl	endline
setprecision	setprecision(n)	specifies the position of decimal in the number having digits.
setfill	setfill(ASCII character);	used to fill blank spaces in a field width.

Header File ctype.h

This file contains the functions for character manipulation. These functions deal with characters.

Various functions used in headerfile ctype.h

1. isalnum
2. isascii
3. isalpha
4. iscontrol
5. isdigit
6. isgraph
7. islower
8. isprint
9. isspace
10. isxdigit
11. ispunct
12. toascii
13. tolower
14. toupper

Function	Syntax	Purpose/Action
1. isalnum	int isalnum (int character);	It tests whether the character alphanumeric. Returns a non-zero value if the character is alphanumeric otherwise zero value.
2. isalpha	int isalpha (int character);	It tests whether the character is alphabetic. Returns a non-zero value if the character is alphabetic, otherwise zero.
3. iscntrl	int iscntrl (int character);	It tests whether the character is control character? Returns non-zero value if the character is a control character otherwise zero.
4. isdigit	int isdigit (int character);	It tests whether the character is a digit. Returns non-zero value if the character is a digit otherwise zero value.
5. islower	int islower (int character);	It tests whether the character is a lower case character. Returns non-zero value if the character is a lower case alphabet otherwise zero value.
6. ispunct	int inspunct (int character);	It tests whether the character a punctuation mark. Returns non-zero value if the character is a punctuation mark, otherwise zero value.
7. isupper	int isupper (int character);	It tests whether the character is a upper case letter. Returns non-zero value if the character is a upper case letter, otherwise zero value.
8. tolower	int tolower (int character);	Returns a character as a lower case if the character is an upper case letter, otherwise returns unchanged.
9. toupper	int toupper (int character);	Returns a character as a upper case if the character is an upper case letter, otherwise returns unchanged.

Character and String Related Functions

(*i*) **isalnum()**

The isalnum() checks whether the argument is alphanumeric or not.

Syntax—

isalnum(x)

Here x is a digit from 0 to 9 or a letter (a to z or A to Z).

It returns True if the argument x is anything in the above digits or letters. It returns False if x is something else than any digit or letter.

The following example illustrates the use of isalnum( ).

```
#include<iostream.h>
#include<ctype.h>
#include<stdio.h>
main()
{
  int x;
     cout<<"Enter Number or Character:";
  x=getchar();
  fflush(stdin);
  if(isalnum(x))
     cout<<"This is a alphanumeric character";
  else
     cout<<"It is not alphanumeric character";
}
```

(*ii*) **isalpha()**

This function checks whether the argument is alphabetic or not. If it is alphabetic (lower case or upper case letter), it returns True, otherwise False.

Syntax—

isalpha(x)

x is any letter in uppercase or lower case. The following example illustrates the use of isalpha().

```
#include<iostream.h>
#include<ctype.h>
main()
{
  char ch;
  cout<<"Enter any character:";
  cin>>ch;
  if(isalpha(ch))
     cout<<"This is an alphabetic character";
```

```
    else
        cout<<"This is not an alphabetic character";
}
```

(iii) **isdigit()**

This function checks whether the argument is a digit from 0 to 9. It returns True if the value is from 0–9 otherwise False.

Syntax—

isdigit(x)

where *x* is any digit from 0 to 9.

```
#include<iostream.h>
#include<ctype.h>
#include<stdio.h>
main()
{
int x;
cout<<"Enter Any Number:";
x=getchar();
fflush(stdin);
if(isdigit(x))
cout<<"This is a digit";
else
cout<<"This is not a digit";
}
```

(iv) **islower()**

This function checks whether the argument is in lowercase or not. It returns True if the argument is a lowercase letter otherwise False.

```
#include<iostream.h>
#include<ctype.h>
#include<stdio.h>
main()
{
    char ch;
    cout<<"Enter character:";
    ch=getchar();
    fflush(stdin);
    if(islower(ch))
    cout<<"It is a lower case letter";
    else
```

```
        cout<<"It is an upper case letter";
    }
```

(v) **isupper()**

This functions checks whether the argument is an uppercase letter or not. It returns True if the argument is a upper case letter otherwise False.

```
#include<iostream.h>
#include<ctype.h>
#include<stdio.h>
main ( )
{
    char ch;
    cout<<"Enter character:";
    ch=getchar();
    fflush(stdin);
    if(isupper(ch))
    cout<<"It is uppercase letter";
    else
    cout<<"It is a lower case letter";
}
```

(vi) **tolower()**

This function converts an uppercase letter to a lowercase letter. If the argument is in lowercase, it returns it unchanged.

Illustration 1 :

```
#include<iostream.h>
#include<ctype.h>
#include<stdio.h>
main()
{
    int ch;
    cout<<"Enter any character:";
    ch=getchar();
    fflush(stdin);
    if(isalpha(ch))
    {
        if(isupper(ch))
        {
            cout<<"This is a lower case letter";
            putchar(tolower(ch));
```

```
            }
        else
            cout<<"This is not an uppercase letter";
        else
        cout<<"This character is not an alphabet";
        }
    }
```

(*vii*) **toupper()**

This function converts a lower case letter to an upper case letter. If the argument is in upper case, it returns it unchanged.

```
#include<iostream.h>
#include<ctype.h>
#include<stdio.h>
main()
{
  int ch;
  cout<<"Enter any character:";
  ch=getchar();
  fflush(stdin);
  if(isalpha(ch))
  {
     if(islower(ch))
     {
        cout<<"This is a uppercase letter";
        putchar(toupper(ch));
     }
  else
     cout<<"This is not a lowercase letter";
  else
  cout<<"This character is not an alphabet";
  }
}
```

SOME OTHER FUNCTIONS

strcpy()

This function is contained in string.h header file. This copies a string into another.

General Syntax—

strcpy(string1, string2)

One string may be called destination string and another as source string.

Illustration: *Write a program using strcpy function to copy the string New Delhi into another string named as str.*

```
//This program determines the use of strcpy()function
#include<iostream.h>
#include<string.h>
main()
{
   chr str[20]; //string str can hold
                 //up to 20 characters.
   cout<<"\n"<<strcpy(str, "New Delhi");
   return 0;
}
```

strcat()

This function is also included in string.h header file. Its function is to append one string (source string) to the end of another string(destination string). The length of string so obtained is equal to the length of both the strings.

General Syntax—

strcat(string1, string2)

Illustration: *Write a program to input a string, to convert the capital letters of the string into small letters and to calculate the total number of vowels in the string.*

Example :

Input	:	*I AM SPIDERMAN*
Output	:	*i am spiderman*
	:	*Total number of vowels : 5*

Solution:

```
#include<iostream.h>
#include<conio.h>
#include<string.h>
#include<stdio.h>
#include<ctype.h>
int main()
{
    int vowel;
    vowel=0;
```

```
char s[50];
int len;
len = strlen(s);
cout<<"Enter the string\n";
gets(s);
cout<<"Input:";
puts(s);
for(inti=0;i<50;i++)
{
  if(isupper(s[i]))
  {
            s[i]=tolower(s[i]);
            }
            }
            cout<<"Output:";
            puts(s);
            for(intj=0;j<50;j++)
            {
                if((s[j]=='a')||(s[j]=='e')||(s[j]=='i')||
                (s[j]=='o')||(s[j]=='u'))
                vowel++;
                }
    cout<<" :Total number of vowels:"<<vowel;
    getch();
    }
```

strlen()

This function is included in string.h header file. This function calculates the length of the string.

General Syntax—

strlen(string)

Illustration: *Calculate the length of the string Educational Publishers using strlen function.*

Solution:

```
//This program illustrates the use of strlen function
#include<iostream.h>
#include<string.h>
main()
{
   char string[]="Educational Publishers";
```

```
    cout<<strlen(string)<<"is the length of string"<<string<<endl;
    return 0;
}
```

strcmp()

This function is also included in string.h header file. This function is used to compare the characters of one string with that of the other.

General Syntax—

strcmp(string1, string2);

strcmp function	returns a value < 0	if string1, string2;
	returns zero value	if string1<string2;
	returns a value > 0	if string1>string2;

Illustration: *Write a program that compares string1(s1) and strings2(s2) given that*

string1 = "Comprehensive"

string2 = "Comprehension"

Solution:

```
//This program illustrates the use of strcmp function and compares
//two string.
#include<iostream.h>
#include<string.h>
main()
{
    char s1[40];
    char s2[40];
    cout<<"Enter first string";
    gets(s1);
    cout<<"Enter second string";
    gets(s2);
    if(strcmp(s1,s2)==0)
    cout<<"\n"<<"string1=string2";
    else
    cout<<"\n"<<"The strings are not equal";
    return 0;
}
```

Run of the Program—

Enter first string SKM

Enter second string SKM

string 1 = string2

MATHEMATICAL FUNCTIONS

abs ()

This functions is included in math.h file. This functions obtains absolute value an integer.

Illustration: *Write a program, using abs functions to absolute value of a given number.*

Solution:

```
//This program obtains the absolute value of a number.
#include<iostream.h>
#include<stdlib.h>
main()
{
    int value=cout<<"\n Enter a number:";
    cin>>value;
    absval=abs(value);
    cout<<"\n"<<"absval="<<absval;
    return 0;
}
```

log 10()

This function is included in math.h file. This function calculates logarithm of the base 10.

Illustration: *To obtain the logarithm to the base 10 of a given number x. Value of x can be placed as 61.3083*

Solution:

```
//This program calculates the logarithm to the base 10 of given number x.
#include<iostream.h>
#include<stdlib.h>
main()
{
    float x,r;
    x=61.3083;
    r=log(x);
    cout<<"\The log to the base 10 is:"<<r<<endl;
    return 0;
}
```

pow()

This function is included in math.h file. This function calculates the value of expression of the form of x^y.

Illustration: *Develop a program using pow function to obtain the value of x^y.*

Take $x = 2.5$

$y = 10$

Solution:

```
//This program uses pow() function to obtain the value of xy
#include<iostream.h>
#include<stdlib.h>
#include<math.h>
main()
{
   float x,y,z;
   x=2.5;
   y=10;
   z=pow(x,y);
   cout<<"\power"<<z<<endl;
   return 0;
}
```

Output of the above program—

9536.743164

sqrt()

This function of math.h header file obtains the square root of the number.

Illustration: *Using sqrt() function, develop a program to obtain the value of 1577.12.*

Solution:

```
//This program calculates the square root of a given number.
#include<iostream.h>
#include<stdlib.h>
#include<math.h>
main()
{
   float x,y,;
   x=1577.12;
   y=sqrt(x);
   cout<<"\sqrt(x)"<<y<<endl;
   return 0;
}
```

sin()

This function of math.h header file calculates the sine of the angle.

Illustration: *Develop a program using sin function to obtain the value of a given angle. Given that value of angle is in radian.*

Solution:

```
//This program obtains the value of a givne angle using sin
//function.
#include<math.h>
#include<iostream.h>
#include<stdlib.h>
main()
{
   float angle, val;
   cout<<"\Enter the angle:";
   cin>>angle;
   val=sin(angle);
   cout<<"\sin of the angle is:"<<val<<endl;
   return 0;
}
```

cos()

This function of math.h header file calculates the cosine of the angle.

Illustration: *Develop a program using cos function to obtain the value of a given angle. Given that—value of angle is in radian.*

Solution:

```
//This program obtains the value of a given angle using cos function.
#include<iostream.h>
#include<math.h>
#include<stdlio.h>
main()
{
   int angle,val;
   cout<<"\Enter the angle:";
   cin>>angle;
   val=cos(angle);
   cout<<"\cos of the angle"<<endl;
   return 0;
}
```

fabs()

This function returns the absolute value of the floating point numbers. This function is derived from math.h header file.

For example fabs (– 123.45) will return 123.45 and fabs (123.45) will also return 123.45.

```
//use of fabs()
#include<iostream.h>
#include<math.h>
main()
{
    float n;
    cout<<"Enter Floating Point Number:";
    cin>>n;
    cout<<"Absolute Value="<<fabs(n)<<endl;
    return();
}
```

fmod()

This function is available in math.h leader file. This function returns the floating point remainder of the fraction say *x*/*y*. *x* and *y* are double data type and the value returned is also of doubled data type.

Illustration:

```
//use of fmod()
#include<iostream.h>
#include<math.h>
main()
{
    double x,y,r;
    x=12.10;
    y=4.5;
    r=fmod(x,y);
    cout<<"The Remainder is="<<r;
}
```

RUN

The Remainder is=3.1

modf()

This function is also of header file math.h. It takes arguments of double data type and splits the value into integer part and fractional part. The integer part is loaded into memory and fractional part is returned.

Illustration:

```
#include<iostream.h>
#include<math.h>
main()
{
    double x,y;
    double r;
    y=4.5;
    r=modf(y, &x);
    cout<<"The Fractional Part is="<<r;
}
```

RUN

The Fractional Part is=0.5

In the above illustration the value of number 4.5 is split. The value 4 is loaded in the memory and fractional part 0.5 is returned.

hypot()

This function returns the value of hypotenuse of a right angle triangle by giving the value of base and perpendicular.

7

FUNCTIONS

INTRODUCTION

A good programmer is capable of creating lengthy program but length of the programs is not of significance if the program is difficult to understand by the other reader or programmer. The capability of the programmer is observed in terms of readable programs created with clear functions and not with lengthy or multiple functions.

It is also for the convenience of programmer himself to make programs with smaller functions and modules. C++ language provides many in-built functions and programmer can use simple or complex functions. But it is always advisable to break a large program to smaller units (known as functions).

WHAT IS A FUNCTION?

A function is a subprogram which can act on data and produce a result. In C++, a function should be defined before its usage in the program.

General Syntax–

```
type function_name(formal-argument list)
```

Every C++ program has at least one main function called main(). When the program starts, the function main() is called automatically and this can call other function/functions but it cannot be called by any other function.

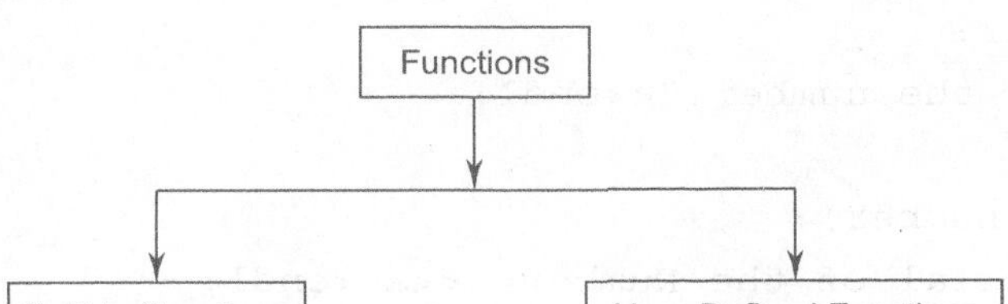

Built-in functions are the part of compiler package and user-defined functions are used according to the requirement of the program.

Some time a function is to be used in various programs, then it is advisable to place this function in a separate header file. When the same function is to be used, the header file is included in the program.

C++ provides various standard header files in which various standard functions are contained. These standard functions are used in the program by writing the name of the functions with appropriate argument (parameter list) which is written within parentheses.

Declaring and Defining a Function

It is essential to first declare the functions in the program and then define it.

The declaration is called Function Prototype and this tells the compiler about name, return type parameters of the function. The function definition tells the compiler how a function works in the program. Many built-in functions have their own prototypes. The files having these prototypes are included in the program by using -

```
#include
```

The definition of a functions consists of the function header. The statements enclosed with in {and} is called the body of the function.

General Syntax—

Type function-name (formal argument list)

```
{ Opening Brace
    Statements                 }
    return expression;         } ——→ Body of the function.
} Closing Brace
```

Illustration: *Write a program which illustrates how to declare a function.*

```
//This program calculates the factorial of a given number using
//function declaration.
#include<iostream.h>
#include<math.h>
main()
{
   int factorial(int);            //Function declaration
   int a, number;
   cout<<"Enter the number."<<endl;
   cin>>number;
   a=factorial(number);
   cout<<"Factorial of the Number="<<a<<endl;
}
```

```
int factorial (int number)
{
   int factorial(int);
   int x=1;
   if(number==1);
   return(x);
   else
   {
      for(int n=1; n<=number;++n)
      x=x*n;
      return(x);
   }
}
```

Run of the Program-

Enter the number: 5

Factorial of the Number is = 120.

Function Prototypes

All functions must be declared well in advance (before use) in a program. The prototype tells the computer about characteristics of the function being used in the program. Many built-in functions have their function prototypes already written. The functions having these prototypes should be included in the program by using #include. In user-defined functions, prototype is included in the source code.

General form-

<type><name>(arguments);

The function prototype is a statement which ends with a semicolon.

There are three main components in function prototype:

1. Function Name
2. Function Type
3. Function Arguments.

Function Name

It is user-defined any legal identifier followed by parentheses without any space.

Function Type

The function type' is the type of value to be returned. Every function has a return type. If a function does not return a value, its return t ype will be void.

Function Arguments

Function arguments is a list of parameters. The arguments (statements) are placed in the parentheses. All function arguments need not be of same type. A function can have integer, character as its arguments. In fact any valid C++ expression may be a function argument which includes constants, logical expressions and other functions that return a value. If the function does not use any argument, the word void is used in the parentheses. Void is a signal to the compiler that no value is to be returned.

The function that does not return a value and that does not require any parameter is declared as follows:

void function-name(parameter list);	does not return a value
type, function name(void);	does not require parameter

Examples of Function Prototypes

void cube_vol();

float volume(int l, float b, float h);

intadd(int a, int b);

Accessing a Function

An accessing function can be called or invoked in/from the main program by using function name, followed by the parameters enclosed in parentheses separated by commas. It is worth nothing that in the function definition in the beginning, the semicolon is not used at the end. If semicolon is absent, it means that you are defining a function and not calling it. Therefore, when a function is called, it is necessary to keep semicolon at the end. A function call statement may be written in the following manner

cube_volume();

This statement will transfer the control to function cube_volume. By using the following statement, we can call the function clear

clear();

It is to be noted that when a call statement is encountered, the control is transferred to the function.

Illustration: *Write a C++ program which illustrates function accessing and prototyping. (You can find the square of the given number).*

Solution:

```
//This program illustrates function accessing and prototyping.
#include<iostream.h>

main()
{
   float square(float);     //function prototype
   float a,b;
   cout<<"Enter the Number\n";
```

```
    cin>>a;
    -b=square(a);
    cout<<"The Square of the Number is="<<b<<endl;
    return 0;
}
float square(float c)
{
    return c*c;
}
```

Run of the Program-

Enter the Number: 5

The Square of the Number is = 25

When the function call statement is given then the control automatically transfers to functions body and statements are executed.

Passing Arguments to Function

In C++ program we can call a function or a number of functions from another function. The various functions can be called from main() function. If the communication between these functions (calling function and called function), is to be made in such a way that there should be not error then the mechanism of using variables from one function to the other should be correct one.

Recursion

A function can also call itself in a process which is called recursion. Recursion may be direct or indirect. When a function calls itself, it is direct recursion and it calls another function, which then calls first function then it is indirect recursion. Sometimes a function uses no parameters (arguments) but it is capable returning a value. For example when we dial telephone No. 100, we do not say anything but from other side a reply is received "Police Control Room". No message is given but information is received. The function which does not use arguments can return a value without giving it any information. It returns the value of first character typed on input medium. *i.e*, keyboard.

The function that have parameters can be accessed in the following ways:

1. Call by Value
2. Call Reference.

Consider the following example:

```
#include<iostream.h>
int main()
{
    int square(int);
    int volume, side=4;
    ..........................................
    ..........................................
```

```
    volume=square(side);
    ........................................
    ........................................
    cout<<volume;                          Invoking of function
    return 0;
}
    int square(int s)
    return s*s;
}
```

The function square() uses the value of side (*i.e.*, 4) here. (call by value)

Illustration: *Program to illustrate the use of call by reference.*

```
#include<iostream.h>
#include<conio.h>
#include<math.h>
main()
{
    void swap(int & ,int &);
    clrscr();
    int x,y;
    x=5,y=10;
    cout<<"The Values before swapping are=\n";
    cout<<"x="<<x<<"y="<<y<<endl;
    swap(x,y);
    cout<<"The Values after swapping are=\n";
    cout<<"x="<<x<<"y="<<y<<endl;
}
void swap(int &a, int &b)
{
    int change;
    change=a;
    a=b;
    b=change;
    cout<<"The values after swapping are";
    cout<<"x="<<a<<"y="<<b<<endl;
}
```

Run of the Program

The Values before swapping are $x = 5, y = 10$

The Values after swapping are $x = 10, y = 5$

The Values after swapping are $x = 10, y = 5$.

Default Arguments

A C++ function prototype can declare that one or more arguments of the function have default values. The default values are specified at the time of function declaration. When a call to the function omits the corresponding parameter argument, the compiler inserts the default values.

A function which does not have explicit return value by default returns a value of type int. The function which does not return a value should declare a return type of void. In C++ program, the function which doesn't indicate a return type returns an integer value.

Example: float interest (float principal, int time, float rat=0.6);

```
comp_int=(6000,3);              //third argument missing
```

The value 6000 passes to the argument principal and value 3 passes to the argument time. Since the third argument for rate is missing, we can use default value 0.6 as rate.

Now if the initialization is done as:

```
comp_int=int(6000,3,0.6);     //no argument is missing
```

here argument principal gets value 6000

argument time gets value 3

and argument rate gets value 0.6

NOTE: It is to be noted until and unless the argument (s) on right side has (have) default, the argument on immediate left cannot have default value.

Study the following declarations

(*i*) float interest(float principal=6000, int time=3, float rate=0.6);

(*ii*) float interest(float principal=6000, int time=3, float rate);

(*iii*) float interest(float principal, int time=3, float rate=0.6);

(*iv*) float interest(float principal=6000, int time, float rate=0.6);

(*v*) float interest(float principal, int time, float rate=0.6);

- First declaration is valid.
- Second declaration is invalid because the right argument has no default but left arguments have default.
- Third declaration is valid because right arguments have defaults. No problem for argument principal because atleast right side arguments (both) have defaults.
- Fourth declaration is invalid because left arguments principal has default value but the right argument time does not have.
- Fifth declaration is valid because only the right most argument has default value.

Constant Argument

Sometimes when arguments are not to be modified in the function, these are declared as constant arguments. If constant values are assigned to the function, then the function is not able to modify the values. Constant arguments are useful when the function is called by reference.

Call by Value

The function which has arguments can be accessed by two ways. One is call value and the other is call by reference. It is better to first know what is actual and formal parameter. Actual parameter means the parameter which happens to be present in a function call statement and formal parameter means the parameter which happens to be in function definition. A call by value method copies the value of actual parameter into formal parameter.

Illustration: *The following program swaps the value of two variables using Call By Value method.*

```
# include< iostream.h>
  void swap (int, int);
  void main()
{
  int x, y;
  cout << "input two numbers" << endl;
  cin >> x;
  cin >> y;
  swap (x, y);
  cout << "In main" <<x<< "" <<y<<endl;
}
  void swap(int Num1, int Num2)
{
  int Temp;
  Temp  = Num 1;
  Num 1 = Num 2;
  Num 2 = Temp;
  Cout<<"In swap" << Num 1 << "" <<Num2 <<endl;
}
```

Call by Reference

Call by reference is frequently used for passing arguments or parameters by reference. Instead of passing a value to the function being called, reference is passed to the original variable. The same variable value can be called by any of the two names, *i.e.*, original variables name and the reference name.

This method is very useful in C++ programs where the original variables are to be changed with others by using a function. When a function receives parameter by reference, the references are attached to the actual arguments provided by the function (calling function).

Call by Value	Call by Reference
Primitive data types are passed by call by value.	Reference data types like objects and arrays are passed by call by reference.
In such process, the method creates new set of variables to copy the value of actual parameter and work with them.	Reference of actual parameters is passed on to the method. No new set of variables is created.
If any change is made in the formal parameter, the same is not reflected in the actual parameter.	Any change made in the formal parameter is reflected in the actual parameter.

Illustration: *Write a C++ program which illustrates passing of arguments reference.*

Solution:

```
//This program illustrates passing of argument by reference.
#include<iostream.h>
#include<stdio.h>
void swap(int &a, int &b)
{
   int x;
   x=a;
   a=b;
   b=x;
}
main()
{
   int i, j;
   i=5;
   j=10;
   cout<<"Values Before Swapping=";
   cout<<i<<endl;
   cout<<j<<endl;
   swap(i,j);
   cout<<"Values After Swapping="<<i<<endl<<j<<endl;
}
```

In this illustration j is the reference and i is the original value.

Some Points to be Noted

1. When a function returns a value in the form of integer (a value of type int) it is called integer function and if it returns the value other than type int (a value of type float), it is called non-integer function.
2. Only variables can be passed in reference and not the constants or expressions.

Return by Reference

A function is capable of returning a reference. Consider the following function

```
int &max(int &a,int &b)
{
    if(a>b)
    return a;
    else
    return b;
}
```

Return type of max() is int &. The function returns reference to *a* or *b*. If we call a function such as max(*x*,*y*), it will give a reference either to *x* or *y* on their values max(*x*,*y*)= – 5

It assigns – 5 to *x* (if *x* > *y*) otherwise – 5 to *y* (*y* > *x*)

Calling Functions with Arrays

When an array is used as argument to a function, the address of the array is passed and not the whole copy of the array. When a function is called with array name, a pointer to the first element in the array is passed into the function.

Computer stores an array into its memory. An array is referred to by its address. It should be noted that passing an array name to a function does not make a fresh copy of the array.

While calling function with arrays the following points be known.

1. The value of elements in the array.
2. The names of elements in the array.
3. The address of the array in memory.
4. The list of address.

The size of array should also be kept in mind. Arrays are one-dimensional, two- dimensional or multi-dimensional. The size of the multi-dimensional array should be specified while there is no need for specification in case of single-dimensional array. The size of array can be very large, but in C++ programming we have only one copy of an array and this is why instead of passing values, only the address of the array is passed.

Illustration: *Write a C++ program to find the sum of values in the array elements.*

Solution:

```
//This program obtains the sum of values in array elements
#include<iostream.h>
#include<stdio.h>
int main()
int sum_arr(int array[],int n)
{
        int total=0;
        for(int i=0; i<n; i++);
        total=total+arr[i];
        return total;
}
int main(void)
{
        int sum[size]={1,8,27,64,125,216,343,512}; //initialization
        int sum1=sum_arr(sum, size);
        cout<<"\Sum of the elements in the array;"<<sum1<<"\n";
        return 0;
}
```

In the above program sum_arr function has been used to find the sum of values. Array has been initialized and uses sum_arr function to calculate the sum.

Returning Values

It has been already discussed that functions return a value. Only the function of type void does not return a value. Void functions are not used as expression.

There are various functions which are used according to the requirement of the program.

Example of functions are cos(), tolower(), toupper, strcpy(), max(), islower() etc.

C++ provides a variety of functions and has a vast library of functions.

Scope Rules of Function and Variables

Sometimes we have to follow some rules which tell us in which part of the program, the identifier or particular data is accessible. Every identifier in the program should be unique so that the particular data could be known and easily accessed. We can use a identifier name more than once in the program but there should be some differentiation in these identifiers.

Class, CLASS and CLasS

are different identifiers and C++ recognizes them as separate identify.

C++ provides 4 kinds of scopes as depicted in the diagram.

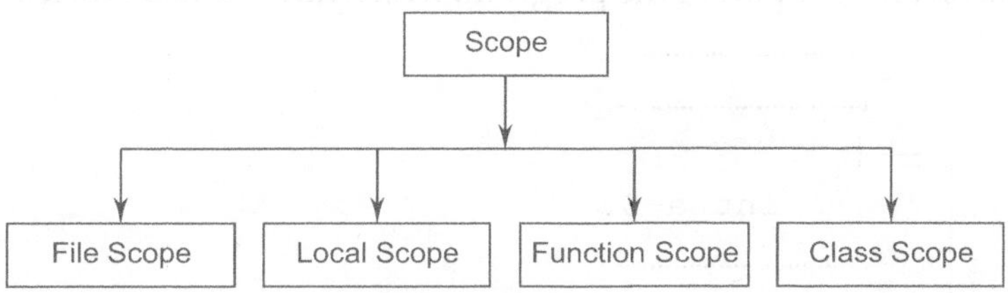

C++ is a block-structured language and scopes can be used in fabricating programs. The scope of variable extends from the point of declaration till the end of block.

1. **File Scope:** When we declare a name outside all block and function, it is called file scope. File scope is the outermost scope of the program.
2. **Local Scope:** A variable declared inside a block is said to be local for that particular block. It can be used only in this block and other sub-blocks contained in that block. A local variable can be accessed only within the function within which it is defined. The argument list is treated as if it was declared in the outermost block of that junction. It is within the local scope of the function. This is not within the enclosing file scope.
3. **Function Scope:** When variables are declared in the outermost block of function, these have function scopes. These variables can be accessed only in that function which has declaration for them.
4. **Class Scope:** The names of class members have class scope. These names are said to be local to the scope of their class. Each class represents a distinct class scope. All member functions are treated as if they were within the scope of their class.

Consider the following program segment

```
..........................
..........................
{
  int a=5;
..........................
..........................
}
..........................
..........................
{
  int a=2;
..........................
..........................
}
```

We have used 2 declarations for 'a' which refer to different memory locations. The statement furnished in the second block cannot refer to the variable 'a' which has been declared in the first block. Similarly the statement furnished in the first block cannot refer to the variable 'a' which is declared in the second block.

Let us have a look on another part of the program, which have nested blocks.

```
                  ..............................
                  ..............................
            ┌──── {
            │           int a=5;
            │     ..............................
            │     ..............................
            │        {              ────┐
Block No.1  │              int a=2;     │
            │              ...........  ├──→Block No.2
            │              ...........  │
            │        }              ────┘
            │     ..............................
            │     ..............................
            └──── }
```

It is visible that Block No. 2 is contained in Block No. 1.

The declaration made in the second block hides a declaration of the same variable 'a' in the outer block. It will refer to different memory locations.

Global and Local Variables

A variable which is defined outside a function is called global variable. A global variable is a variable to all the functions which are defined in the file. Global variables, throughout the execution, hold their values. Global variables can be accessed from within any function if it is declared properly otherwise it cannot be accessed. The use of global variables however results in complexity but they produce faster code.

In contrast to global variables, local variables are defined within a function. A local variable can have the same name as the global variable has. In such a situation when the name of local variable is same as of global variable, the function hides the global variable.

Function Overloading

C++ allows to write a program with a number of functions with the same name but different arguments and return type. This property is called function overloading.

Example:

```
include<iostream.h>
int sum (int a, int b)          //function to add two integers
{
   return(a + b);
}
float sum (float a, float b) //function to add two float variables
{
   return (a + b);
}
void man()
{
   int n=2, n1=5, r1;
   float x=5.00, y=6.00,r2;
   r1=sum(n, n1);
   r2=sum(x, y);
   cout<<"r1="<<r1<<"r2="<<r2<<endl;
}
```

SOME MORE WORKED-OUT EXAMPLES

1. Write the output of the following program:

```
#include<iostream.h>
void execute(int &B, int &C = 100)
{
    int TEMP=B+C;
    B+=TEMP;
    if(C==100)
       cout<<TEMP<<B<<C<<endl;
    {
       int M=90, N=10;
```

```
        execute(M);
        cout<<M<<N<<endl;
        execute(M,N);
        cout<<M<<N<<endl;
    }
}
```

Solution:

190	280	100
280	10	
570	10	

2. What will be the output of the following program:

```
#include<iostream.h>
static int i=100;
void abc()
{
    static int i=8;
    cout<<"first="<<i;
}
main()
{
    static int i=2;
    abc();
    cout<<second="<i<<endl;
}
```

Solution:

first=8 second=2

3. Write a user defined function in C++ to display the sum of column elements of a two dimensional array.

Solution:

```
void addition(int R[7][7])
{
    int a,b;
    int total;
    total=0;
    for(a=0;a<7;a++)
    sum=0;
    for(b=0;j<7;b++)
    {
      total=total+R[a][b];
    }
    cout<<"The sum of elements is="<<total;
}
```

8

CLASSES AND OBJECTS

OBJECT ORIENTED PROGRAMMING

Object oriented programming is concerned with re-usable and modifiable software. OOP has been developed to increase programmer's productivity to overcome the traditional programmming. C++ provides an indispensable object oriented programming facilitates to the programmer in solving the problems with the available software of OPP. Features of the OOP have been shown in the following figure.

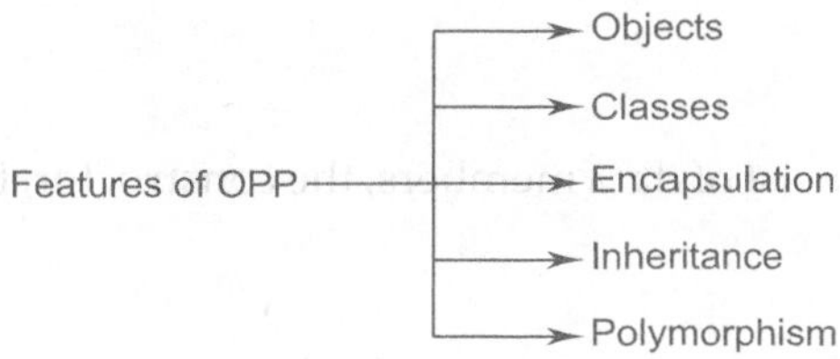

OBJECTS

An object is a type of data which is a self contained unit containing data, codes and the member functions which can operate on data. The object is meaningful in the context of solving of a problem. The object may be an item, place, person or any other thing.

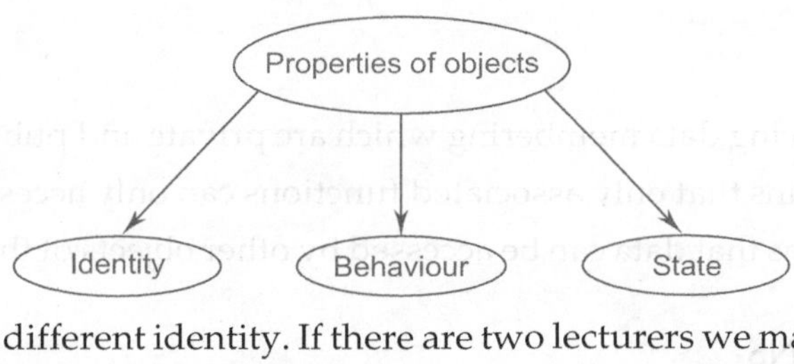

Two objects may have different identity. If there are two lecturers we may treat them same object. However, their function is same as of teaching but one may be Physics Lecturer and the other English

Lecturer. Two books may not be said the same object by merely looking but these are the properties which help identify them. One book may be of Physics and the other on Computers.

Objects Declared as Classes

A class is a collection of objects. It is a user-defined aggregate data type. It contains both data members and function members. A class may be defined as a group of objects with same operations and attributes. The 'class' is a key concept in C++ and is a user defined type. The class is a mechanism which supports data abstraction by allowing representation details through a set of operations defined as a part of class. In OPP, a programmer deals with classes and not with individual objects.

In short we can say that class is an abstract data type to store both data and related functions together. The main aim of using the class is to hide data and functions from the external world. The main concept of OPP is also data hiding.

Example

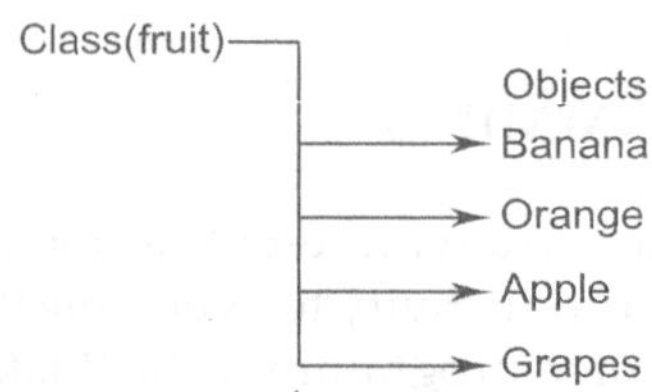

Banana, Orange, Apple, Grapes are distinct objects but these belong to fruit class.

The objects belonging to a class are called **instances of the class**.

Class Members

A class has members which consist of data members, the constructor, function, destrcutor functions and member functions.

Data Members

A class member may be any valid C++ data type. For example the 'Cone' class has the following data members.

Visibility of Class Members

Visibility of class members is accessed by the two access specifiers.

1. Private class
2. Public class

The cone has the following data membering which are private and public.

The private access means that only associated functions can only access the data.

The public access means that data can be accessed by other objects of the program.

MEMBER FUNCTIONS

Member functions of the class are those functions which are declared within the class. These functions are given suitable codes.

Simply speaking, the functions which indicate the kind of operation that can be performed on given data are known as member functions. Member functions are sometimes referred to as 'Methods'.

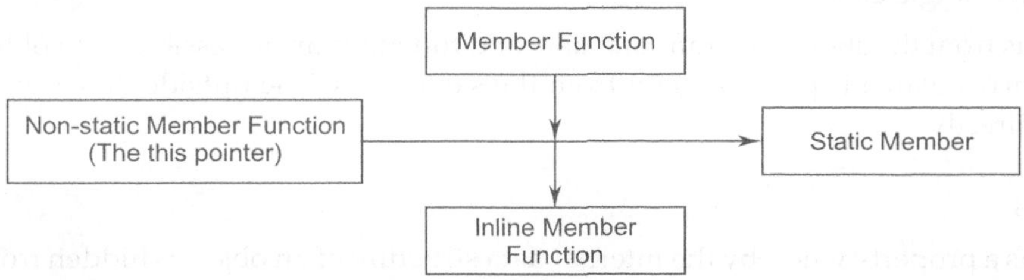

Non-Static Member Functions

In a non-static member function, the keyword "This" is pointer to the object.

Inline Member Functions

Inline member functions may be defined in the class declaration. When a function is defined within a class it becomes equivalent to declaring it in-line.

Static Members

Static member functions can use only the names of static members and enumerators. A data may be declared as static in class declaration. A static member is not a part of objects of a class. There is only one copy of static data number which is shared by all objects of the class in C++ program.

ENCAPSULATION

Encapsulation is a fundamental concept of OOP. Before defining encapsulation, it is better to understand what is structure.

A structure is an aggregate (sum total) of data type. The structure contains integers, pointers, arrays, unions, floats and other valid and meaningful data. Encapsulation is addition of functions to structures into an independent entity called object. By adding functions to strcutures, the ability of structure increases and it includes algorithms which work with other structure members.

Encapsulation helps the programmer in concentrating on the relevant details. Encapsulation makes the classes independent and these can be reused without modifications in other program.

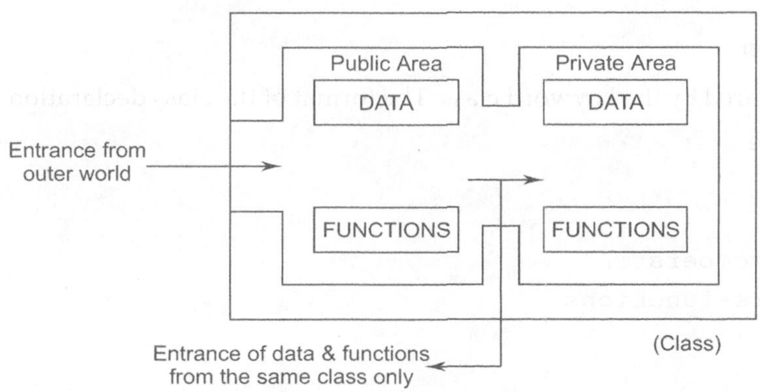

The data declared inside a class are called data members and functions declared in a class are called function members or member functions. Encapsulation is a technique to bind related data and functions into a single class.

It is obvious from the above diagram that data and functions are accessible from outer world but the entry to private area is possible only from the same class. The outside data cannot enter the private area directly.

Data Hiding

Data Hiding is a property whereby the internal data structure of an object is hidden from rest of the program. Data hiding is achieved by declaring object numbers under private section of a class.

Example

```
class Employee
{
    int empno;
    char name[30];   ---->  These data members are hidden
    double salary;          from outside world.
  public:
    void detdata();
    void showdata();
}
```

Creating an Object

After declaration of a class, an object can be created like any other variable using the class name as type specifier. In case, if a class is already defined, you can define the variables similar to structures.

The syntax of defining the object is given below:

```
class_name object_name;
```

If you want to define three similar objects x, y, z you can write

number x, y, z;

Where number is a class name and x, y, z are three constructed objects having the class structure number.

Class Declaration

A class can be declared by the keyword class. The format of the class declaration is as under:

```
class sample
{
   private:
      data-members
      members-functions
   public:
```

```
        data-members
        member-functions
    protected:
        data-members
        member-functions
}
```

The class name sample used above, uses three access specifiers like private, public and protected to their respective data members and member functions.

At one look class declaration is similar to a structure declaration but it has both data and function as its members instead of only data members.

Properties of Classes

1. Classes allow both private and public members.
2. Classes consist both data and functions.
3. A private member is not accessible outside the class, but a member function can access such a member.
4. A member functions defined inside the class is by default an inline function.
5. A member functions can be overloaded.
6. Objects can be passed as parameters to functions and returned from a function.

Member Function Definition

Member function can be defined both inside and outside the class declaration. Sometimes, a member function is very small. This small function can be defined inside the class itself.

Consider the following class declaration:

```
class student
{
    private:
int a;
    public:
        void readdata()
        {
        cin>>a;
        }
    void writedata()
    {
    cout<<a;
    }
};
```

Two public functions `readdata()` and `writedata()` have been defined in the class. In case of a large member function, it is defined outside the class definition.

Points to note for Making a Function Inline

A function can be inline if:

-- it is very small.

-- it is not recursive.

-- it does not contain static variables.

-- it does not contain any loop.

-- it does not contain return statement.

Consider the following case, in which member function definition is outside *i.e.* class declaration.

```
class student
{
    private:
        int a;
    public:
        void readdata();
        void writedata();
    };
    void student::readdata()
    {
    cin>>a;
    }
    void student::writedata()
    {
    cout<<a;
}
```

In the above program segment, a function has been defined from outside the related class.

The general syntax can be given as

```
returntype class_name::function_name (arguments)
```

returntype can have any value like void, int, float etc.

The operator :: is known as scope resolution operator which is used while defining a function from outside the class.

Consider the following examples

The following functions has been written to convert Fahrenheit to Centigrade.

```
float temp::farne(float F)    //Declaration of function
{
    C=(F-32)*5/9;
    return(C);
}
```

It should be noted that variable F and C are private and function farne () is public. This function has been used to convert fahrenheit into centigrade. This function can be called as member function. This member function is defined outside the class by qualifying the function name with the class name.

Illustration: *The following program illustrates the use of member function.*

```
#include<iostream.h>
#include<math.h>
class addiff
{
   float a,b;
   public:
   void readdata(void);
   void showdata(void);
};
void addiff::readdata()
{
   cout<<"Enter First Number:";
   cin>>a;
   cout<<"Enter Second Number:";
   cin>>b;
}
   void addiff::showdata(void)
{
   float x,y;
   x=a+b;
   y=a-b;
   cout<<"Sum of the Numbers is="<<x;
   cout<<"Difference of the Numbers is="<<y;
}
   void main(void)
{
   addiff;              //objects defined as having the class addiff.
   readdata();          //execute the class function readdata()
   s.showdata();        //Execute the class function showdata()
                        //end of function main()
```

Array within a Class

Arrays can be used as data members in a class. A class member may contain an array and in the same way a set of classes may also be kept in an array. The method of usigng an array in a class is exactly similar to the use of array with structures.

The following illustration is explained to show the usage of arrays in the class.

Illustration: *A school stores the records of its 40 teachers using an object array. Each object follows a class and the data members of the class are:*

name, subject, pay, allowance and totalpay.

[pay, allowance and total pay are the members of private data]

Write a C++ program to accept data of each member of object array and to show the name and subject of the teachers whose total pay exceeds Rs. 10000 per month.

Solution:

```
#include<iostream.h>
class teacher
{
   float bpay, all, totpay;
   public:
     char name[30];           //use of array in member
     char subj[20];
     void readdata(void);
     void showdata(void);
};
void teacher::readdata(void)
{
     cout<<"\n Enter the name of the teacher:";
     cin>>name;
     cout<<"\n Enter the Subject of the Teacher:";
     cin>>subj;
     cout<<"\n Basic pay of the Teacher=";
     cin>>bpay;
     cout<<"\n Allowances of the Teacher=";
     cin>>all;
     totpay=bpay+all;
     }
void teacher::showdata(void)
{
   if (totpay>10000)
   cout<<"Name of the Teacher:"<<name<<endl;
   cout<<"Subject of Teaching:"<<sub<<endl;
   }
   void main(void)
   {
```

```
    teacher tc[30];
    int i;
    for(i=0; i<3; i++)
    {
        cout<<"Enter Data:"<<i+1;
        tc[i].readdata();            //calling the array of objects
    }
    cout<<"Name of Teachers whose total pay more than 10000:";
    for(i=0; i<3; i++)
    tc[i]showdata();                 //calling array of objects
    }
```

Arrays of Objects

Like declaring arrays of common data types, you can declare arrays of class objects.

```
worker man[15];
```

The above declaration creates an array of 15 worker objects. The array *max* calls the class objects 15 times to input worker data 15 times and prints them.

Illustration: *Consider a class student with the following specification:*

Data members of class student

name (20 characters)

roll (2 digit)

avg (floating point with 2 decimal places)

Member function of `class student getdata()` *function to accept values for the data members.* *showdata* () *function to display the data members on the*

Declare the class student:

Define an array object of type student with 10 members, locations write a function is C++ initarray () *to initialise the array objarr.*

Solution:

```
class student
{
    private:
    char name[20];          //private data members
    float roll;             //which can be
    float avg;              //accessed by member functions
    public:
      void getdata();
      void showdata();
};
```

```
        void student::getdata()
{
        int validinput=0;
        cout<<"\n Enter Name:";
        cin>>name;
do
    {
        cout<<"\n Enter Roll Number:";
        cin>>roll;
        if((roll<0)||(roll>99))
        cout<<"\n Invalid input!"<<endl;
    else
        validinput=1;
}
        while(!validinput);
        cout<<"Average Score:";
        cin>>avg;
}
void student::showdata()
{
    cout<<"\n Enter Name:"<<name;
    cout<<"\n Roll Number:"<<roll;
    cout<<" Average Score:"<<avg<<endl;
}
student objarr[10];                  //Defining an array objarr
void initarray(student objarr[]) //function initarry
{
    int n;
    for(n=0; n<=10; n ++)
{
    cout<<"Serial Number:"<< i<<endl;
    objarr[i].getdata();
}
}
```

Nesting of Member Functions

A member function of a class can be called by another member function of the same class. It is a must that new member function should belong to the same class. This is known as nesting of member function.

Illustration: //This program modifies the basic pay of workers by adding 1.58 times to their basic pay.

```
#include<iostream.h>
#include<conio.h>
#include<math.h>
class worker
    {
float bpay[100];
        int i,n;
        void showdata();
    public:
        void readdata();
        void add();
    };  //readdata, add are two functions & belong to same class.
void worker :: readdata()
    {
        cout<<"\n Enter the length of data=";
        cin>>n;
        cout<<"\n Enter the basic pay=";
          for(i=0,i<n;i++)
          cin>>bpay[i];
    }
    void worker :: add()
    {
        for(i=0;i<n;i++)
        bpay[i]=bpay[i]+bpay[i]*1.58;
        showdata();          //Calling the member function showdata
    }
    void worker :: showdata()
    {
        for(i=0;i<n;i++)
        cout<<bpay[i];
        cout<<endl;
    }
        void main()          //declare object data of class workers
    {
        data.readdata();  //calling the object member function
                                  readdata() from main
        data.showdata();  //calling the object member function
                                  showdata() from main
    }
    }
```

Objects as Function Arguments

Different types of data can be used as function arguments. An object can be passed to a function as an argument.

Normally there are two methods for passing variables:

(*i*) Pass by value

(*ii*) Pass by reference

Pass by Value

If we pass a copy of the entire object to a function, it means pass by values. The objects are passed to a function by value. Actual object is not received by the function.

Consider the following program segment:

```
void main(void)
{
    worker a;
    a.inputdata("Bihari Lal", 3000);           //Pass by value
    a.showdata();
}
```

In the above segment `a.inputdata (.....)` passes the private data members into member functions of worker class.

Illustration:

```
//This program illustrates the passing of variables by value.
#include<iostream.h>
#include<conio.h>
#include<stdlib.h>
#include<string.h>
class Employee
{
public:
char name[30]; //Data Members
double salary:
float DA;
float HRA;
//Member Function inside
void inputdata(char ename[25], double slry); //the class with scope
                         //resolution operator.
                         //Function inputdata() is a pass by value
void inputdata(char ename[30], double slry);
```

```
void outputdata(Employee temp);
void calculate(Employee temp);
void calda(Employee temp);
void calhra(Employee temp);
void calgross(Employee temp);
};
void Employee::inputdata(char ename[25], double slry)
{
strcpy(name,ename);
salary=slry;
}
void Employee::outputdata(Employee temp)
{
cout<<"Employee Name"<<temp.name;
cout<<"Basic Salary"<<temp.salary;
}
void Employee::calda(Employee temp)
{
DA=0.8*temp.salary;
cout<<"DA is"<<DA;
}
void Employee::calhra(Employee temp)
{
HRA=0.10*temp.salary;
cout<<"House Rent"<<HRA;
}
void Employee::calgross(Employee temp)
{
double GROSS;
GROSS=temp.salary+temp.HRA+temp.DA;
cout<<"Gross Salary is"<<GROSS;
}
main()
{
clrscr();
Employee emp, temp;
temp.inputdata("Ramu", 3500);  //Function object passes
                               //values to inputdata class function
```

```
temp.output data(temp);
temp.calda(temp);
temp.calhra(temp);
temp.clagross(temp);
}
```

Output of the Program

Employee Name	Ramu
Basic Salary	3500
DA is	2800
House Rent	350
Gross Salary is	6850

Pass by Reference

Sometimes, it is required that the changes made to an object in the called function should reflect back into the calling function. This is done with the help Pass by Reference Method. The address of an object is passed to the function of an argume. The address of the Object is shown by preceding the object name with the character *'e'*.

Illustration:

```
//This program illustrates the use of Passing Variable by Reference.
#include<iostream.h>
#include<conio.h>
#include<stdlib.h>
#include<string.h>
class Employee
{
public:
char name[30];
double salary;
void inputdata(char ename[30],double slry);
};
void Employee::inputdata(char ename[30], double slry)
{
strcpy(name,ename);
salary=slry;
}
main()
{
clrscr();
```

```
float HRA, DA, GROSS;
Employee temp;
temp.inputdata("Ramu", 3500);
Employee &emp=temp;          //passing value by reference at main()
cout<<"Employee Name"<<temp.name;
cout<<"Basic Salary"<<temp.salary;
DA=0.8*temp.salary;
cout<<"DA is"<<DA;
HRA=0.10*temp.salary;
cout<<"House Rent"<<HRA;
GROSS=temp.salary+HRA+DA;
cout<<"Gross Salary is"<<GROSS;
}
```

Scope Resolution Operator(::)

The Scope Resolution Operator (::) is represented by double colon (::) used to connect the definition of functions to their classes. It is used in those situations where a global variable exists with the same name as a local variable. To use a member function outside the class, the scope resolution operator : is used.

Syntax

```
        return type<classname>::<function_name>(parameter_list)
```

Illustration 1: *What will be the output of the following program?*

```
#include<iostream.h>
int a=20;
void main()
{
    void demo(int &, int, int*);
    int a=40,b=10;
    demo(::a,a,&b):
    cout<<::a<<a<<b<<endl;
}
void demo(int &x, int y, int*z)
{
    a+=x;
    y*=a;
    *z=a+y;
    cout<<x<<y<<*z<<endl;
}
```

Output of the Program

40 16001640

40 40 1640

Illustration 2: *Consider the class declaration class FLIGHT*

```
{
   int flight_no;
   char destination[20];
   float distance;
   public:
   void INPUT();        //To read an object from the keyboard
   void Write_File(); //To write N objects 1 into a file, where N is
                             passed as argument
   void OUTPUT(); //To display the file contents on the monitor
};
Complete the member functions definitions.
```

Solution:

```
class FLIGHT
{
   int flight_no;
   char destination[20];
   float distance;
   public:
   void INPUT();
   void Write_File();
   void OUTPUT();
};
void FLIGHT::INPUT (FLIGHT F)
{
   cout<<"The flight information:";
   cin>>F.flight no;
   cin>>F.destination;
   cin>>F.distance;
void FLIGHT::Write_File(int n)
   {
      ofstream outfile;
      outfile open(record.dat", ios::app);
      FLIGHT F;
      for(int i=1; i<=n; i++)
```

```
      {
         cout<<"flight no:"<<i;
         INPUT(F);
         outfile write((char*) &F, size of (F));
      }
   }
   void FLIGHT::OUTPUT(void)
{
   ofstream infile;
   infile.open("record.dat");
   infile.seekg(0);
   FLIGHT F;
   while(!infile.eof())
   {
      infile.read((char*) &F, sizeof (F));
      cout<<"Flight-information";
      cout<<F.flight_no;
      cout<<F.destination;
      cout<<F.distance;
   }
}
```

Illustration 3. *Consider the class declaration*

```
class BUS
{
   int bus_no;
   char destination[20];
   float distance;
   public:
   void Read();   //To read an object from the keyboard
   void Write(); //To write an object into a file
   void Show();   //To display the file contents on the monitor
};
```

Complete the member functions definitions.

Solution:

```
class BUS
   {
      int bus_no;
      char destination[20];
```

```
        float distance;
        public:
          void Read();
          void Write();
          void Show();
    };
void BUS::Read(void)
{
   cout<<"Enter Bus no";
   cin>>bus_no;
   cout<<"destination of the bus";"
   cin>>destination;
   cout<<"distance between destinations";
   cin>>distance;
}
void BUS::Write(void)
{
   ofstream outfile;
   outfile open("Record.dat", ios::app);
   file.write((char*)this sizeof(*this));
}
void BUS::Show(void)
{
   ifstream infile("Record.dat", ios::in);
   infile.seekg(0);
   while(linfile.eof())
   {
      infile.read(char*) &b, sizeof (b));
      cout<<"information of bus:";
      cout<<bus_no<<" "<<destination<<" "<< distance;
   }
}
```

Illustration 4: *Define a class **worker** with the following specification:*

Private members of class **worker**

`wno`	integer
`wname`	25 characters
`hrwrk, wgrate`	float(hours worked and wage rate per hour)
`totwage`	float(hrwrk*wgrate)

calcwg() A function to find hrwrk*wgrate with float return type

Public members of class **worker**

in_data() a function to accept values for wno, wname, hrwrk, wgrate and invoke **calcwg()** to calculate totpay.

out_data() a function to display all the data members on the screen.

You should give definitions of functions.

Solution: A complete program for calculation of wages has been given below:

```
//This program calculates the wages of workers.
#include<iostream.h>
#include<dos.h>
#include<conio.h>
#include<stdio.h>
class worker
{
   private:
   into wno;
   charwname[25];
   float hrwrk, wgrate;
   float totwage;
   float calcwg()
   {
      return(hrwrk*wgrate);
   }
   public:
   void in_data();
   void out_data();
};
void worker::in_data()
{
   cout<<"Enter the Worker-Number:"<<endl;
   cin>>wno;
   cout<<"Enter the Name of Worker:"<<endl;
   gets(wname);
   cout<<"Enter the Number of Hours:"<<endl;
   cin>>hrwrk;
   {
      if(hrwrk>9)
    wgrate=12;
```

```
        else wgrate=10;
    }
    totwage=calcwg();
}
void worker::out_data()
{
    cout<<"The Worker-Number of the Worker:"<<wno<<endl;
    cout<<"The Name of the Worker:"<<wname<<endl;
    cout<<"Total Wages Earned by the Worker:"<<totwage<<endl;
}
void main()
{
    worker s;
    cout<<"Enter Values:"<<endl;
    s.in_data();
    s.out_data();
    getch();
}
```

Output of the Program

Enter Values:

Enter the Worker-Number:

515

Enter the Name of Worker:

RAJKUMAR

Enter the Number of Hours:

7

The Worker-Number of the Worker: 515

The Name of the Worker: RAJKUMAR

Total Wages Earned by the Worker: 70

Illustration 5. *A class student has three data members-NAME, ROLLNO, MARKS of the following subjects and member function to ASSIGN STREAM on the basis of table given below:*

Average Marks	*Stream*
91% or more	*Physics*
86%—90%	*Electronics*
81%—85%	*Chemistry*
76%—80%	*Mathematics*
71%—75%	*Computer Science*

Declare the class STUDENT and define the member function.

Solution:

```
class STUDENT
{
   private:
   char NAME[30];
   int ROLLNO;
   float MARKS[5];
   char STREAM[20];
   void ASSIGN()
}
void STUDENT::ASSIGN()
{
   float SUM=0, AVERAGE;
   for(int i=0;i<5; i++)
   SUM +=marks[i];
   AVERAGE=SUM/5;
   if(AVERAGE>=91.00)
      strcpy(STREAM, "Physics");
   else if(AVERAGE>=86.00)
      strcpy(STREAM, "Electronics");
   else if(AVERAGE>=81.00)
      strcpy(STREAM, "Chemistry");
   else if(AVERAGE>=76.00)
      strcpy(STREAM,"Mathematics");
   else if(AVERAGE>=71.00)
      strcpy(STREAM, "Computer Science");
   else strcpy(STREAM, None);
}
```

Illustration 6: *Give the output of the following program:*

```
#include<iostream.h>
#include<string.h>
class per
{  char name[20];
   float salary;
   public:
   per(char *s, float a)
   {  strcpy(name,s); salary=1;}
   per*GR(per & x)
```

```
    {  if(x.salary>=salary)
   return &x;
       else
           return this;
    }
    void display()
    {  cout<<"Name:"<<name<<"\n";
    cout<<"Salary":<<salary<<"\n";
    }
};
void main()
{  per P1("REEMA", 10000), P2("KRISHNAN", 20000),
    P3("GEORGE", 5000);
    per *P;
    P=P1.GR(P3); P->display();
    P=P2.GR(P3); P->display();
}
```

Solution:

The OUTPUT will be as under:

Name	:	REEMA
Salary	:	10000
Name	:	KRISHNAN
Salary	:	20000

A financial institution has only two kinds of accounts; Simple and Compound. A class Account has two protected attributes account Number(a positive integer) and principal(a double precision real number to store the money deposited initially). The interest for a simple account is calculated by using the simple interest formula:

$$SI = PRT/100$$

Where SI-Simple interest, P-Principal, R-Rate of interest per annum T-Time in years

The interest for a compound account is calculated by using the compound interest formulae:

$$CI = P[1 + R/100]^{T} - P$$

Where CI-Compound interest, P-Principal, R-Rate of interest per annum, T-time in years. Rate and Time for two kinds of accounts may vary.

Model the above situation by defining classes Account, Simple and Compound where Simple and Compound are Derived classes from the Class Account.

Write appropriate constructors for passing various attributes for the three classes.

Write the functions double interest() that calculates the appropriate interest and returns the interest for the classes simple and compound.

Also write the functions display() for the three classes which prints out all the attribute values as

Account Number = ______________________

Principal = ______________________

Rate = ______________________

Time = ______________________

Interest = ______________________

With each attribute on a single line. Make sure that each display() function is correctly placed in the appropriate class. You need not write the main function.

Solution:

```
class Account
{
   protected:
   int an;
   int p;
   public:
   Account(int accn, int pri)
   {
      an=accn;
      p=pri;
   }
   void readdata()
   {
      cout<<"\n Enter the account number:";
      cin>>an;
      cout<<"\Enter the principal deposited:";
      cin>>p;
   }
   void display();
   {
      cout<<"\n account number is:" <<an;
      cout<<"\n principal is:"<<p;
   }
}
class simple::public Account
{
   double rate;
   in time;
   public:
   simple(int accn,double pri,double r,int t)
```

```
    {
       rate=r;
       time=t;
    }
    double interest()
    {
       return((p*Rate*time)/100);
    }
    void display()
    {
       Account::display();
       cout<<"\n Rate"<<rate;
       cout<<"\n Time"<<time;
    }
    class compound::public Account
    {
       int time;
       int rate;
       public;
       compound(int accn,double pri,double r,int t)
       {
          rate=r;
          time=t;
       }
       double interest()
       {
          return(p*pow(1+rate/100),(double)(time)-principal);
       }
       void display()
       {
       Account::display();
       cout<<"\n Rate"<<rate;
       cout<<"\n Time"<<time;
    }
}
```

9

POINTERS

POINTER

A pointer helps in accessing data by indirect reference. The basics of the pointers and different aspects associated with them are discussed below.

POINTER DECLARATION

A pointer is a variable which holds a memory address of another variable in the memory. It is to be noted that each variable is located at a certain location in the memory. This location is called address.

All pointers, when they are created, should be initialized to some value. The value may even be zero. The pointer having zero value is called null pointer.

```
int*pAge=0;
```

Here pAge is a pointer to int. pAge holds the address of an int. Pointer plays an important role in programming with the following advantages.

1. It supports dynamic allocation/deallocation of memory.
2. It provides various functions to modify their calling arguments.
3. It allows to pass arrays, strings, functions as function arguments.
4. Pointer helps in swapping the variables without their physical movement.
5. Pointer helps in improving the efficiency of certain routines.
6. Access data members and functions.

General syntax of pointer declaration-

```
data-type*pointer-variable;
```

The Indirection Operator(*)

Indirection means to access the value at the address held by the pointer. A pointer provides the programmer an indirect way to read the value held at the address.

The indirection operator is called a dereference operator and represented by *(asterisk) with a variable. When a pointer is dereferred, the value stored at the address by the pointer can be retrieved. It is to be kept in mind that *(asterisk) must be preceded by pointer variable as given in the following examples.

```
int*pAge;
char*pName;
double*pIntt;
```

The Address Operator (&)

The address operator is represent by '&' and is used to get the address of variable. The address operator & is a unary operator and returns the memory address of its operand. When a variable *'a'* is declared in the program, a storage location *'a'* becomes available in the memory.

```
int a;
a=2;
```

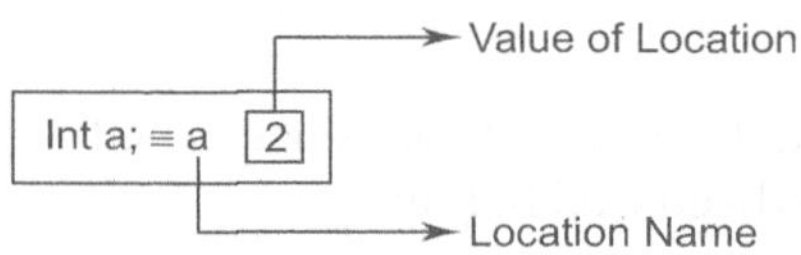

Illustration: *Write a simple C++ program which demonstrates the use of address operator '&'*

Solution:

```
//This program demonstrates the use of address operator &
#include<iostream.h>
main()
{
   int a;
   a=6;
cout<<"\Address of Memory Location is:"<<&a;
}
```

DYNAMIC ALLOCATION OPERATORS

You have read in previous article that when a variable is declared, a storage location is created to the program.

```
int a;
a=6;
```

`int a; ≡ a 6`

When a C++ program is compiled, the computer's memory breaks down into four zones:

1. Program's code
2. Global Data
3. Stack
4. Heap

The allocation of memory at the time of compilation is referred to as static memory allocation. Dynamic variables can be allocated memory according to the needs of a running program. The allocation of the memory at the run time is referred to as Dynamic Memory Allocation.

NEW

The key word new calls upon the function operator new() to obtain new memory space.

General Syntax—

```
data-type*pointer-name = new data-type;
```

The data type can be char, int, float or array etc.

The **new int** tells the program that some new storage space is required for holding this int. The new operator looks for the number of bytes required and needs memory.

Illustration:

```
//This program illustrates the use of New Dynamic Operator
#include<iostream.h>
main()
{
    int *ptrl;
    ptrl=new int;          //allocates dynamic memory
    *ptrl=20;
    cout<<"\Enter the number.";
    cin>>*ptrl;
    *ptrl=*ptr+1;          //incremental value
    cout<<"\The Incremental value is:"<< *ptrl;
    delete ptrl;           //returns the dynamic memory
    return 0;
}
```

DELETE

The delete operator removes the variable space which was occupied by new operator dynamically.

General Syntax—

```
delete ptr;
```

Illustration:

```
//This program illustrates the use of Delete operator
#include<iostream.h>
main()
{
    int*hisAge;
```

```
    hisAge=new int;             //allocation of new memory space
    *hisAGE=25;
  cout<<"\Enter his age";
  cin>>*hisAge;
  *hisAge=*hisAge+1;
  cout<<"\His age next year will be "<<*hisAge;
  delete hisAge;                //Return the dynamic memory
  return 0;
  }
```

POINTERS AND ARRAYS

In C++, pointers and arrays are closely related to each other. Arrays may be single; two multidimensional. It is the notable characteristic of the array that the first element in the array is numbered 0. The elements of the array are stored in contiguous memory locations. Initialization is another important characteristic of array.

The pointer is a variable which can appear on the left side of the assignment, whereas the array is constant and it does not appear on the left side of assignment operator. The difference in the pointer and array is due to this the property otherwise they are similar in all other aspects.

Pointers and One-Dimensional Arrays

Pointers and One-Dimensional Arrays are closely associated with each other as consider the following case:

```
int digit[12];
int *pointer;
```

The array variable digit is an array type. The address of the first element can declared as digit [0]. The digit [0] holds the address of zeroth element of the. The pointer variable 'pointer' as given above is also an address to digit[0].

Consider other cases:

1. pointer = &digit[0];
   The address of zeroth element has been assigned to pointer variable 'pointer'.
2. pointer++==digit[1];
   pointer+5==&digit[5];
   *pointer==digit[];

Illustration: *Write a C++ program which displays the contents of array.*

Solution:

```
//This program displays the contents of array.
#include<iostream.h>
main()
{
```

```
        static int x[6]={6,1,3,0,8,3};
        int j,k, temp;
        k=6;
        cout<<"\The Contents of the array are:";
        for (j=0;j<=k-1;++j)
        {
           temp=*((x)+(j));
           cout<<"Digit is"<<temp;
        }
}
```

Pointers and Multidimensional Arrays

You have seen that the pointer to an array contains the address of first element.

Consider the following cases:

(*i*) & digit[0] (*ii*) & digit[0][0]

The case (*i*) is an example of single dimensional array and case (*ii*) is that of two dimensional array. Consider the following case:

pointer + 1 = &digit[0][1]

Here, the pointer variable has been incremented to the next data element.

ARRAYS OF POINTERS

Like any other data type, the pointers may be arranged. All the rules which are applicable to a simple and ordinary array are applicable to the array of pointers. An array of the pointer contains a collection of address likewise a pointer variable. Consider the following example:

int *pointer[5];

means

pointer[0] pointer[1]......pointer[5]

	0	1	2	3	4
Array Pointer					

Consider the following case:

int *x*[15], *y*[25], *z*[40];

int *pointer[80];

In this case pointer is an array of pointers which is used to point the first elements of arrays x, y and z.

Illustration: *Write a C++ Program which displays the contents of an array of pointers.*

Solution:

```
//This program displays the contents of an array of pointers.
#include<iostream.h>
```

```
main()
{
    int *ptr[4];              //array of 4 int pointers declared
    int a, b, c, d;
    a=6;
    b=1;
    c=30;
    d=83;
    ptr[0]=&a;
    ptr[1]=&b;
    ptr[2]=&c;
    ptr[3]=&d;
    for(int j=0; j<4; j++)
    cout<<"\The contents of the pointer are:"<<*(ptr[j]);
}
```

POINTERS AND STRINGS

A string is a one dimensional array of characters. A string is terminated by all character *i.e.*, '\0'. The constants of the string are written in double quotes.

"RAJNISH" is a string of 8 characters.

R
A
J — 8 Characters (last being '\0')
N
I
S
H
'\0'

By using pointers, we can compare, concatenate, copy strings.

Illustrations: *Write a C++ program which counts the number of characters in a given string.*

Solution:

```
//This program counts the number of character in a given string.
#include<iostream.h>
#including<string.h>
#define max 100
main()
{
```

```
    char string[100];
    void show_data(char*ptr);
    int n;
    cout<<"\Enter the String:";
    cin.get(string, max, '\n')
    cout<<"\The contents of the string:";
    show_data(string);
    n=str_length(string);
    cout<<"The number of characters"<<n;
}
void show_data(char *ptr)
{
    while(*ptr!=null)
    {
        cout<<*ptr;
        ptr++;
    }
}
```

2. *Write a C++ program which copies one string into another.*

Solution:

```
//This program copies one string into another.
#include<iostream.h>
#define max 100
main()
{
    char S1[max], S2[max];
    void show_data(char *pt);
    void strcopy(char *new, char *source);
    cout<<"\Enter String:";
    cin.get(S1, max);
    cout<<"\Contents of string one:";
    show_data(S1);
    strcopy(S2, S1);
    cout<<"\Contents of String two:";
    show_data(S2);
}
void strcopy(char*new, char *source)
{
    while(*source!=null)
```

```
        {
            *new=*source;
            new++;
            source++;
        }
        *new++='\0;
    }
    void show_data(char*pt)
    {
        while(*pt!=null)
        {
            cout<<*pt;
            pt++;
        }
    }
```

Reference

Reference is an alias. When you create reference in the C++ program, the program initialises the reference with the name of another object (destination or target object). Any change made to the reference directly affects the object. Reference operator (&) is used in reference. The reference operator (&) uses the same symbol as of Address Operator.

Consider the following case:

```
int &Ref=some;
```

'Ref' is a reference to the integer which has been initialized to refer to 'some'.

Illustration: *Consider the following program.*

Solution:

```
#include<iostream.h>
main()
{
    int digit;
    int &Ref=digit;
    digit=6;
    cout<<"\digit:"<<digit<<endl;
    cout<<"\Ref:"<<Ref<<endl;
    Ref=9;
    cout<<"\digit:"<<digit<<endl;
    cout<<"\Ref:"<<Ref<<endl;
}
```

The output of the program will be:

digit: 6

Ref: 6

digit: 9

Ref: 9

Functions

A function is a subprogram which can act on data and produce a result. In C++, the function should be defined before its usage in the program.

Pointers are frequently used in function declaration. Functions can be easily represented by pointers and their access is possible. A function can be invoked in two ways.

Call by Value

The function which have arguments can be accessed by two ways. One is called by value and the other is call by reference. It is better to first know what is actual and formal parameter. Actual parameter means the parameter which happens to be present in a function call statement and formal parameter means the parameter which happens to be in function definition. A call by value method copies the value of actual parameter into formal parameter.

Illustration: *Write a C++ program which swaps the value of two given numbers.*

Solution:

```
//This program swaps the values of two given numbers.
#include<iostream.h>
main()
{
    int a;
    int b;
    void swap(int,int);
        a=745756;
        b=613083;
    cout<<"\Values before swap:";
    cout<<"\a="<<a;
    cout<<"\b="<<b;
    swap(a,b);                          //call by value
    cout<<"\Swapped values:";
    cout<<"\a="<<a;
    cout<<"\b="<<b;
}
void swap(int a, int b)
{
```

```
    int temp;
   temp=a;
   a=b;
   b=temp;
}
```

Input of the program	Output-
a = 745756	a = 613083
b = 613083	b = 745756

Call by Reference

Call by reference is frequently used for passing arguments or parameters by reference, instead of passing a value to the function being called, reference is passed to the original variable. The same variable value can be called by any of the two names *i.e.*, original variables name and the reference name.

This method is very useful in C++ programs where the original variables are to be changed with others by using a function. When a function receives parameter by reference the references are attached to the actual arguments provided by the function (calling function).

When a pointer is passed to a function, the address of the data item is passed to that function. This address can be freely accessed. If any change is made in the data of that address, it will be available both in the function and calling part of the program.

Illustration: *Let us again take the case of swapping the contents.*

Solution:

```
#include<iostream.h>
main()
{
    int a;
    int b;
    void swap(int*a, int*b);
       a = 745756;
       b = 613083;
    cout<<"\Value before swap:";
    cout<<"\a="<<a;
    cout<<"\b="<<b;
    swap(&a, &b);                    //call by Reference
    cout<<"\swapped values:";
    cout<<"\a="<<a;
    cout<<"\b="<<b;
}
void swap(int*a, int*b)
```

```
{
    int temp;
    temp=*a;
    temp=*b;
        *a=*b;
        *b=temp;
}
```

Input of the program

$a = 745756$
$b = 613083$

Output-

$a = 745756$
$b = 264998$

Pointers and Objects

An object is an instance of class which can be used as a function argument similar to any other data type. Pointers and objects have also relationship with each other. A pointer can point to an object created by a class.

Bird parrot;

Here Bird is a class and parrot is an object of class Bird.

Bird *ptr;

Here pointer*ptr is of the type Bird.

We can access an object of class variable by pointer as per following syntax

1. (*object-name).member-name = variable;
2. object-name → member-name = variable;

Class-Type

A pointer variable may be declared as a member to a class as per requirement in a C++ program. Consider the following program segment:

```
Class odd_Number
{
    private:
    int x;
    int y;
    public:
    void inputdata();
    void outputdata();
}
odd_Number*ptr;
```

In this program segment*ptr is a pointer variable. This holds the address of class odd_Number. Two data members are int x and int y.

Arrow Operator (→)

The arrow operator is represented by →

Syntax-

object-name → member-name = variable;

The arrow operator points to the member of a class.

Illustration: *Consider the following program.*

Solution:

```
#include<iostream.h>
class emp_inf
{
   private:
   long int pf_no;
   char sex;
   public:
   void inputdata();
   {
      cout<<"\PF number:";
      cin>>pf_no;
      cout<<"\sex:";
      cin>>sex;
   }
   void showdata()
   {
      cout<<"\PF Number:"<<pf_no;
      cout<<"\sex:"<<sex;
   }
};
void main()
{
   emp_inf*ptr;
   cout<<"\Enter Information:";
   ptr→inputdata();
   cout<<"\Class Contents:";
   ptr→showdata();
}
```

This Operator

The pointer this is used to represent an object which invokes a member function.

Illustration: *Consider the following program.*

Solution:

```
#include<iostream.h>
class Number
{
   private:
   int x;
   int y;
   public:
   inline void outputdata();
};
inline void Number::outputdata()
{
   this->x=20;
   this->y=24;
   cout<<"\Number x:<<this->x;
   cout<<"\Number y:<<this->y;
}
void main(void)
{
   Number a;
   a.outputdata();
}
```

The output of the program will be

```
           Number x: 20
           Number y: 24
```

10

CONSTRUCTORS AND DESTRUCTORS

CONSTRUCTOR

A constructor is a special member function which is automatically called when an instance of the class is created. The task of the constructor is to initialize the objects of its class. Initialization combines the definition of the variable with its initial assignment. The name constructor is because it constructs the values of data members of the class.

Rules for Writing Constructor Function

1. It may not be static and virtual.
2. It is declared with no return type.
3. A constructor should have public or protected access within the class.

General Syntax—

```
class Number
{
    int a;
    int b;
    public:
    Number(void);
}
Number::Number(void)
{
    a=0;
    b=0;
}
```

Characteristics of Constructor Functions

1. They may have default arguments like other C++ programs.
2. Their address cannot be referred to.

3. They do not return values not even void.
4. They make implicit calls to the operators new and delete when we require memory allocation.
5. They are automatically invoked with the creation of objects.
6. Constructors cannot be virtual.

Illustration: *Write a C++ Program to generate Fibonacci Series using constructor.*

Solution:

```
// This program generates Fibonacci Series using constructor.
#include<iostream.h>
class Fib_Series
{
   private:
   unsigned long int a0,a1,a2;
   public:
   Fib_Series()                    //Constructor
   {
     a0=0;
     a1=1;
     a2=a0+a1;
   }
   void incremental_value()
   {
     a0=a1;
     a1=a2;
     a2=a0+a1;
   }
   void showdata()
   {
     cout<<a2:";
   }
};
void main(void)
Fib_Series x;
for(intj=0;j<=10;++j)
{
   x.showdata();
   x.incremental_value();
}
```

Default Constructors

A default constructor is a special member function which initializes the data members of a class with no arguments. It is optional to define the default constructor in the program. If it is not defined, the compiler automatically generates it in the program.

General Syntax—

```
class Number
{
   protected:
   ..........................
   ..........................
};
   private:
   ..........................
   ..........................
   public:
   Number();                    //default constructor
   ..........................
   ..........................
};
   Number::Number()
{
}
```

Illustration:

```
//This program illustrates the use of default initialization of a
constructor.
#include<iostream.h>
class emp_inf
{
   private:
   char emp_name[30];
   long int pf_no;
   char sex;
   public:
   emp_inf();                   //constructor
   void showdata();
};
emp_inf::emp_inf()
{
```

```
    emp_name[0]='\0';
    pf_no=0;
    sex='\0';
}
void emp_inf::showdata()
{
    cout<<"Name of Employee:\n"<<emp_name;
    cout<<"PF Number:\n"<<pf_no;
    cout<<"sex:\n"<<sex;
}
void main()
{
    emp_inf a1;
    cout<<"Demonstration of Default Constructor";
    a1.showdata();
}
```

Parameterized Constructors

The constructors which can take arguments are referred to as parameterized constructors. Sometimes we have to initialize different data elements of different objects with different values when the objects are created in C++ programs. This can be done by passing arguments to the constructor function with the creation of objects.

Consider the following program segment:

```
class Number
{
    int a;
    int b;
    public:
    Number(void);
    ..................................
    ..................................
};
Number::Number(void)          //Declaration of Constructor
{
    a=0;
    b=0;
}
```

In this example the data members *a* and *b* have been initialized to a zero value.

If we want to assign different values to these data members, the segment will be as follows:

```
class Number
{
    int a;
    int b;
    int a1, b1;
    public:
    Number(int a, int b) //parameterized constructor
    ..............................
    ..............................
};
Number::Number(int a, int b)
{
    a1=a;
    b1=b;
}
```

Copy Constructors

A copy constructor is used to create a temporary object of a class object. The copy constructor can do the following things:

1. It can initialize and declare one object by another object of the same class. The process of initialization through a copy constructor is called copy initialization.
2. It can return objects as a function value.

General Syntax—

```
class-Name::class-Name(class-Name &ptr)
```

A copy constructor takes a reference to an object of the same class as an argument and produces such object.

Illustration:

```
//This program demonstrates the use of copy constructor.
#include<iostream.h>
class Fib_Series
{
    private:
    unsigned long int n,n1,n2;
    public:
    Fib_Series()
    {
      n=0;
      n1=1;
```

```
    n2=n+n1;
  }
  Fib_Series(Fib_Series &ptr)
  {
    n=ptr.n;
    n1=ptr.n1;
    n2=ptr.n2;
  }
  void incremental_value()
  {
    n=n1;
    n1=n2;
    n2=n1+n2;
  }
  void showdata()
  {
    cout<<n2;
  }
};
void main(void)
{
  Fibr_Series x;
  for (int j = 0; j<10; j++)
  {
    x.showdata();
    x.incremental_value();
  }
}
```

Constructor Overloading

Constructor overloading simply means to declare the method (function) with the same name as that of class to construct objects. C++ allows the use of different functions with the same name (as that of class) and different arguments.

Illustration:

```
class Test
{
  char Paper[20];
  int marks;
```

```
    public:
    Test()                      //constructor1
    {
      strcpy(Paper,"Computer");
      marks=0;
    }
    Test()                      //constructor2
    {
      strcpy(Paper, P);
      marks=0;
    }
    Test (int M)                //constructor3
    {
      strcpy(Paper,"Computer);
      marks=M;
    }
    Test(charP[ ], int M)  //constructor4
    {
      strcpy(Paper, P)
      marks=M;
    }
};
```

Destructors

You have learnt by now that a constructor creates object. A destructor is function which is used to destroy the objects created by a constructor. The main use of the destructor is to create space in the memory. A destructor does not take any argument and it does not return any value.

Characteristics of a Destructor Function

1. It does not return any value not even void.
2. Destructor function does not take any argument, therefore, it cannot be overloaded.
3. The destructor function name is the same as the class name but it is preceded by a tilde (~). For example -number() {}
   Here, the destructor for the class number has been represented.
4. It must have public access in the class declaration.

General Syntax—

```
class Number
{
    private:
```

```
    .........................
    .........................
    protected:
    .........................
    .........................
    public:
    .........................
    .........................
    Number();                //constructor
    ~Number();               //destructor
};
Consider the following case:
#include<iostream.h>
class emp_inf
{
    private:
    char name[30];
    long int pf_no;
    char sex;
    public:
    emp_inf();//constructor
    ~emp_inf();//destructor
    void inputdata();
    void showdata();
};
```

Illustration: *Identify the syntax error (s), if any (giving reason for error):*

```
class ABC
{ int x=10;
  float y;
  ABC() {y=5;}
  ~ABC() {};
};
void main()
{
  ABC a1,a2;
}
```

Solution:

Errors

int *x*=10; is wrong. It cannot initialize class member.

ABC *a*1, *a*2; is wrong. Destructor for ABC is not accessible,

*a*1 is assigned a value that is never used.

11

INHERITANCE

INHERITANCE

Inheritance is a technique which is used to derive or build new classes from existing one to build object oriented hierarchy. A class may be derived from one or more classes.

The new classes are called derived classes and the existing one is called base class.

The derived class inherits the properties of its base class including its member functions and structures with multiple inheritance, a derived class may have more than one base class and each of which may have one or more base classes of its own.

The derived class can add its member functions and data members. It is capable of overriding the member functions of the base.

Usefulness of Inheritance

1. Data in existing class can be modified. Developed software can be created.
2. Object oriented hierarchy can be built.
3. Cost of software can be reduced.

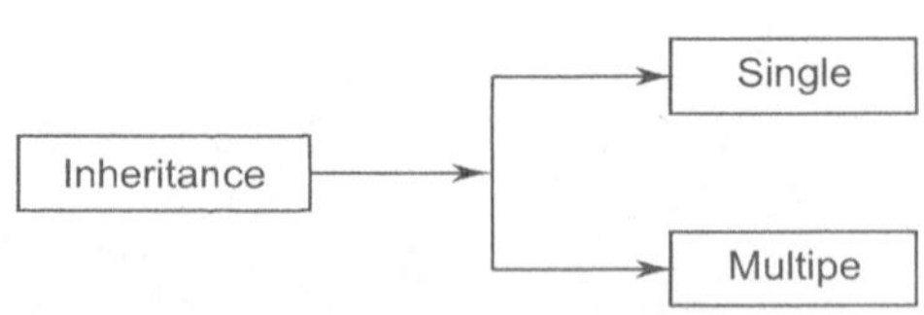

Hybridization means added properties to base class.

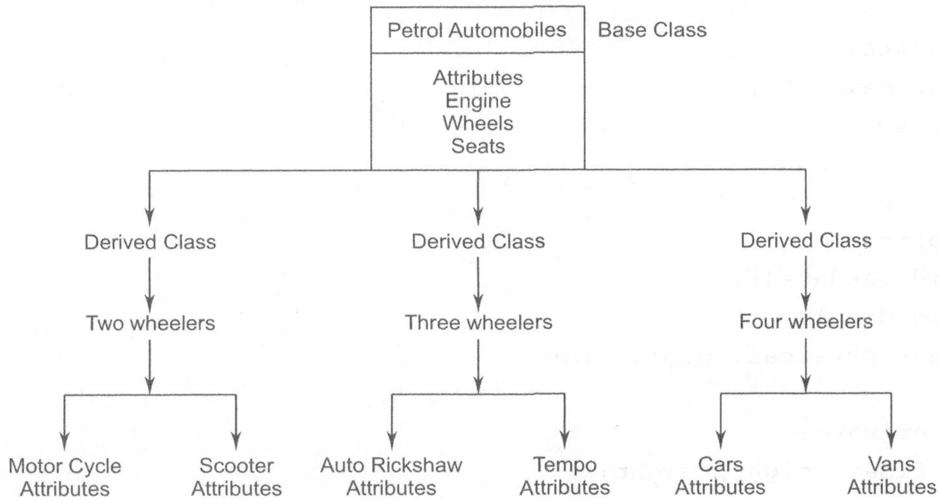

(Concept of Inheritance)

Single Inheritance

When a derived class derives properties from one base class, it is called single inheritance. Simply, single inheritance is the property of creating new classes from an existing base class.

The existing class is called direct base class and the new class is called Singly derived class. A derived class can be defined by specifying the relationship with the base class in addition to its own details.

General Syntax of the derived class—

class derived-class name: private/public/protected base-class-name

A derived class contains the following essential components:

1. the keyword class
2. derived class name
3. colon
4. type (private, public or protected)
5. name of base class

The single colon indicates that the derived-class name has been derived from the base class name.

```
private:
...//
public:
....//data members
...//protected:
....//data members
```

The visibility mode is optional. The visibility may either be private or public.

```
class inf
```

```
{
   private:
   char name[30];
   int age;
   long int r_no;
   char sex;
   public:
   void getdata();
   void display();
   class physical: public inf
   {
      private:
      float weight,height;
      public:
      void getd();
      void disp();
   }
```

Illustration: *Write a C++ program which demonstrates single inheritance.*

Solution:

```
//This Program demonstrates single inheritance.
#include<iostream.h>
#include<iomanip.h>
class emp_inf
{
   private:
   char emp_name[30];
   long int pf_no;
   char sex;
   public:
   void inputdata();
   void outputdata();
};
void emp_inf::inputdata()
{
   cout<<"\n Enter Employee Name:";
   cin>>emp_name;
   cout<<"\n Enter PF Number:";
   cin>>pf_no;
```

```
    cout<<"\n Enter Employees's sex:";
    cin>>sex;
}
void emp_inf::outputdata()
{
    cout<<emp_name<<" ";
    cout<<pf_no<<" ";
    cout<<sex<<" ";
}
void main()
{
    emp_inf x;
    cout<<"\n Enter Information:";
    x.inputdata();
    cout<<"\Emp Name            PF No        Sex";
    cout<<"\_________________________________";
    x.outputdata();
    cout<<"\_________________________________";
}
```

Types of Base Classes

A class can be a base class and the class which is derived may be the base of another class.

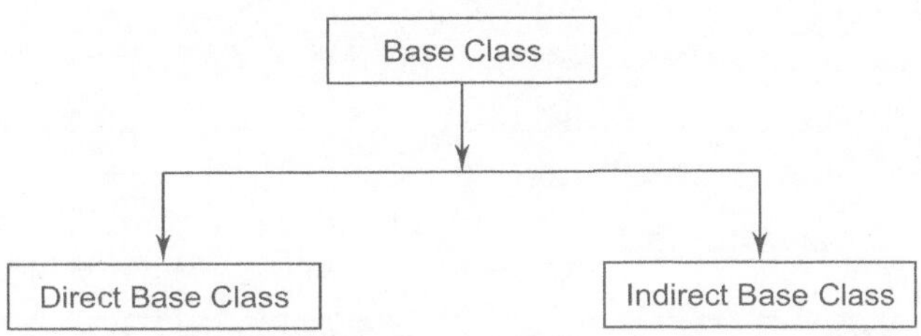

Direct Base Class

Consider the following program segment:

```
class baseX
{
..............................
..............................
};
class derivedX1: public baseX
{
```

```
    ...................................
    ...................................
}
```

In this program segment class baseX is a direct base class.

Consider another program segment

```
class baseX
{
...................................
...................................
}
class baseX1
{
...................................
...................................
};
class baseX2
{
...................................
...................................
};
class baseX3
{
...................................
...................................
};
class baseX4
{
...................................
...................................
};
class derivedY:    public baseX, public baseX1, public baseX2
                     public baseX3, public baseX4
{
...................................
...................................
};
```

Here the derived classY can be derived from any number of base class.

Indirect Base Class

Let us have a look on the following diagram:

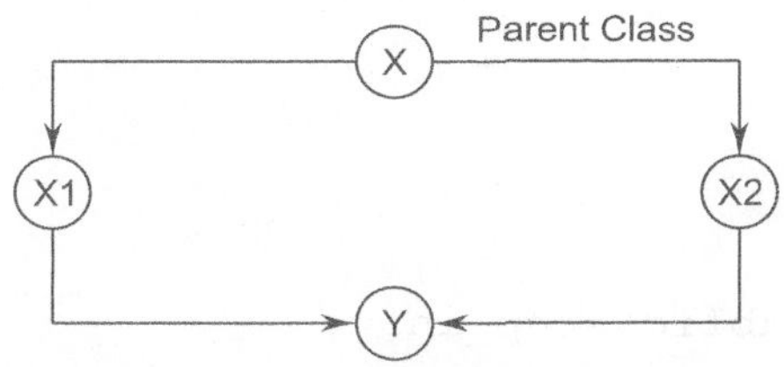

In this diagram Y can inherit the properties of parent class X via two direct base class X1 ind X2. X can be considered as indirect base class.

The following program segment illustrates the concept of indirect base class:

Example

```
class baseX
{
....................................
....................................
};
class derivedX1: public baseX
{
....................................
....................................
};
class derivedX2; public derivedX1
{
....................................
....................................
};
```

Here the class derivedX1 is an indirect base class of the class derivedX2.

Illustration: *Write a C++ program which explain single base class and two derived classes (using the concept of single inheritance).*

Solution:

```
//This program explains the concept single base class and two
//derived classes using single inheritance.
#include<iostream.h>
#include<iomanip.h>
class emp_inf
{
   private:
```

```
    char emp_name[30];
    long int pf_no;
    char sex;
    public:
    void inputdata();
    void showdata();
};
class fund_amount: public etnp_inf
{
    private:
    float pf_loan;
    float pf_cont;
    public:
    void inputdata();
    void outputdata();
};
class loan_inst: public emp_inf
{
    private:
    float installment;
    float periodicity;
    public:
    void inputdata();
    void outputdata();
};
cout<<"\n Enter Employee Name:";
{
    cin>>emp_name;
    cout"\n Enter PF Number:";
    cin>>pf_no;
    cout<<"\n Enter Employee Sex:";
    cin>>sex;
}
void emp_inf::outputdata()
{
    cout<<emp_name<<" ";
    cout<<pf_no<<" ";
    cout<<sex<<" ";
}
```

```
void fund_amount::inputdata()
{
   emp_inf::inputdata();
   emt cout<<"\n Enter PF Loan"
   cin>>pf_loan;
   cout<<"\n Enter PF contribution:";
   cin>>pf_cont:
}
void fund_amount::outputdata();
   cout<<set precision(2);
   cout<<pf_Joan<<a";
   cout<<pf count<<"*;
}
void loan_inst::inputdata()
{
   emp_inf::inputdata();
   cout<<"\n Enter Amount of Installment:";
   cin>>installment;
   cout<<"\n Enter periodicity of Installment";
   cin>>periodicity;
}
void loan_inst::outputdata()
{
   emp_inf::outputdata();
   cout<<installment<<" ";
   cout<<periodicity<<" ";
}
void main()
   fund_amount a;
   loan_inst b;
   cout<<"\n Enter the data for Provident Fund:";
   a.inputdata();
   cout<<"\n Enter the data for Loan Installment:";
   b.inputdata();
   cout<<"\n Provident Fund against total contribution:";
   cout<<"\"*;
   cout<<"Emp_Name PF_No Sex pf_loan pf_cont";
   cout<<"\___________________________________";
   a.outputdata();
```

```
    cout<<endl;
    cout<<"\_";
    cout<<endl;
    cout<<"\Information Regarding Installment";
    cout<<"\";
    cout<<"TEmp_Name PF_No Sex Installment Periodicity";
    cout<<"\ ";
    b.outputdata();
    cout<<endl;
    cout<<"\";
}
```

Visibility Modes

You have so far seen that inheritance is a process of creating a new class from the existing one. A visibility mode specifies the way in which the properties of the base class are derived. A derived class can have one of the following access specifies:

(*i*) Public Inheritance
(*ii*) Private Inheritance
(*iii*) Protected

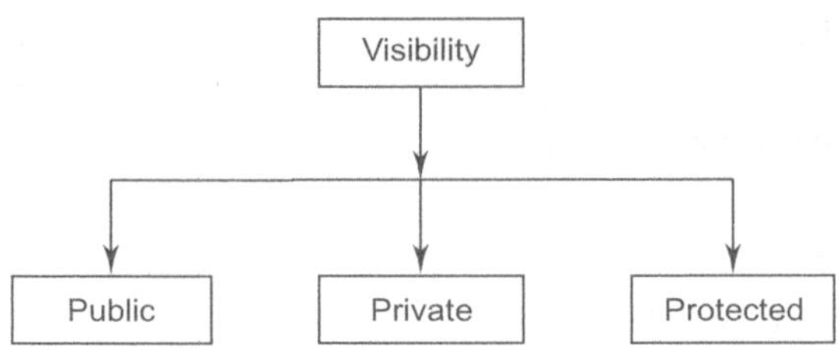

Public Inheritance

Public derivation is one of the most important access specifiers in C++ programming.

When the base class is publicly inherited, the public members of the base class become public member of the derived class.

In public inheritance the following rules should be remembered upon.

(*a*) Each protected member of the base class is protected in the derived class.
(*b*) Each public member of the base class is public in the derived class.
(*c*) Each private member of the base class remains private in the private class.

There is no need to define the inherited members in the derived class.

General Syntax—

```
class base-class-name
{
```

```
    ____________________
    ____________________
}
class derived class-name: public base-class-name
{
    ____________________
    ____________________
}
```

Consider the following example:

```
class Parent
{
    private:
    int a;
    public:
    int b:
    protected:
    int c;
};
class Child: public Parent
{
    private:
    int d;
    public:
    int e;
    protected:
    int f;
};
```

Here the derived class Child has been derived from base class Parent.

The derived class Child has inherited the public data member b and protected data member c from the Parent Class and private member a remains private in the base class Parent.

Private Inheritance

Private derivation means that the base class has been inherited privately.

In private inheritance, the following rules be remembered upon.

(*a*) Public members of the base class are private in the derived class.

(*b*) Protected members of the base class are private in the derived class.

(*c*) Private members of the base class remain private in the base class. These are only visible in the base class.

It is to be noted that members so inherited in the derived class can be accessed only through member functions of the derived class. Further, if the derived class is the base class of any other class, these inherited members cannot be further inherited.

General Syntax—

```
class base-class-name
{
class derived-class-name: private base-class-name
{
    ________________
    ________________
}
Consider the following program segment:
class Parent
{
    private:
    int a;
    public:
    int b;
    protected:
    int c;
};
class Child:private Parent
{
    private:
    int d;
    public:
    int e;
    protected:
    int f;
};
```

Protected Inheritance

Protected Inheritance means that the deprived class can access private and public members of the base class protectedly. In protected inheritance, the following rules should be remembered upon:

(*a*) Protected members of the base class are protected in the derived class.

(*b*) Public members of the base class are protected in the derived class.

(*c*) Private members of the base class remain private. These are visible only in the base class.

General Syntax—

```
class base-class-name
{
```

```
    _______________
    _______________
}
class derived-class-name: protected base-class-name
{
    _______________
    _______________
}
Consider the following program segment.
class Parent
{
    private:
    int a;
    public:
    int b;
    protected:
    int c;
};
class Child: private Parent
{
    private:
    int d;
    public:
    int e;
    protected:
    int f;
};
```

ACCESS CONTROL

You have seen by now, how the members of the class can be accessed. Public, Private and Protected derivation clearly exhibit the access mechanism in C++ programming. Let us discuss in detail how the data (public, private and protected) can be accessed. There are three types of access controls.

1. Access control in Publicly derived class.
2. Access control in Privately derived class.
3. Access control in Protectedly derived class.

Accessing Publicly Derived Data

The public members of the class can be accessed by the following;

(*a*) Member functions of the class.
(*b*) Member functions of the friend class.
(*c*) Non-Member functions of the class.
(*d*) Member functions of the derived class (if the class has been publicly derived).

Consider the following examples:

Example 1.

```
class Publishers : public Text_Books
{
   public:
   int i;
   void inputdata();
   void outputdata()
   {
      ++i;
   }
};
```

In this program segment, the member function of the class can access the public data.

Example 2.

```
class Publishers : public Text_Books
{
   public:
   int i;
   void inputdata()
};
class Books : public Publishers
{
   public:
   void outputdata()
   {
      ++i;
   }
};
```

In this program segment, the public data can be accessed by the derived class, if the data has been derived publicly.

Accessing Privately Derived Data

Private members of a class can be accessed by the following:-

(*a*) Member functions of the class.
(*b*) Member functions of the friend class in which it is declared.

Illustration: *Write a C++ program that demonstrates the access of a private member.*

Solution:

```
//This program demonstrates the access of a private member.
#include<iostream.h>
class Books
{
   private:
      int sales;
   public:
      Books()
   {
      cout<<"\n Enter Sales:";
      cin>>sales;
   }
};    //end of base class declaration
class Maths  : public Books
{
   public:
   void outputdata()
   {
      ++sales;
      cout<<"\n Sales of Mathematics Books="<<sales;
   }
};
void main()
{
   Maths a;
   a.outputdata();
}
```

Accessing Protectedly Derived Data

The protected data members of a base class can be accessed by the public member function of the derived class. The protected data members can be accessed by the following:

(*a*) Member Function

(*b*) Friends of the class in which it is declared.

It is to be noted that member function of the class so derived can be accessed by the member functions irrespective of the fact whether it has been derived privately, provided the derived class as a direct base.

Consider the following program segment:

```
class Books
{
   protected:
   int sales;
};
class Physics : private Books
{
   public:
   void main()
   {
      ++sales;
   };
}
```

In this program segment the data member of Books (Base Class) can be accessed by the public member function even if it has been privately derived, provided the derived class Physics has a direct base.

Illustration: *Write a C++ Program which demonstrates the access of a protected member.*

Solution:

```
//This program demonstrates the access of a protected member.
#include<iostream.h>
class Books
{
   protected:
      int sales:
   public:
      Books()
   {
      cout<<"\n Enter Sales:";
      cin>>sales;
   }
};    //end of base class declaration
class Chemistry : private Books
{
   public:
   void outputdata()
   {
      ++sales;
```

```
        cout<<"\n Sales of Chemistry Books="<<sales;
    }
};
void main()
{
    Chemistry a;
    a.outputdata();
}
```

Multiple Inheritance

When a derived class derives properties from more than one base class, it is called multiple inheritance.

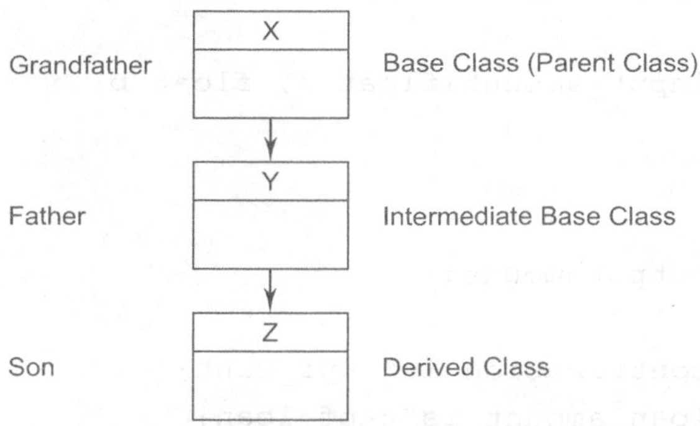

In C++ programming a derived class from base class can also become base class for other derived class.

It is obvious from the diagram that X is the parent class. Y has been derived from X and Z has been derived from Y. Y in this case serves as intermediate base class and Z is recent most derived class. Simply, we can say that X is grandfather, Y is Father and Z is son. The chain X-Y-Z is called inheritance path. The inheritance of this type is called multilevel inheritance. This process can continue to any number of levels.

```
class Employee
{
    protected:
        int pf_no;
    public:
    void inputdata(int);
    void outputdata(void);
};
void employee :: inputdata(int x)
{
    pf_no = x;
```

```
}
void employee :: outputdata()
{
   cout<<"\n Provident Fund Number:"<<pf_no;
   class pf_detail::public employee  //First Level of Inheritance
   {
      protected:
         float pf_cont;
         float pf_loan;
      public:
         void inputamount(float, float);
         void outputamount(void);
};
void pf_detail::input_amount(float a, float b)
pf_count=a;
pf_loan=b;
}
void pf_detail::outputamount()
{
   cout<<"\n PF contribution is"<<pf_cont;
   cout<<"\n PF loan amount is"<<pf_loan;
}
class pf_amount::public employee //Second Level of Inheritance
{
   float net_pf;
   public:
   void showdata(void);
}
void pf_amount::showdata(void)
   net_pf=pf_count-pf_loan;
   outputdata();
cout<<"\Net PF amount is"<< net_pf;
main()
pf_amount employee1;
   employee1.inputdata(3303);
   employee1.inputdata(35600,20000);
   employee1.showdata();
}
```

The output of the program will be

Provident Fund Number: 3303

PF Contribution is 35600

PF loan is 20000

Net PF amount is 15600

We can generate further details in similar manner.

Multilevel Inheritance

When a new class is derived from more than one base class, it is called multiple inheritance.

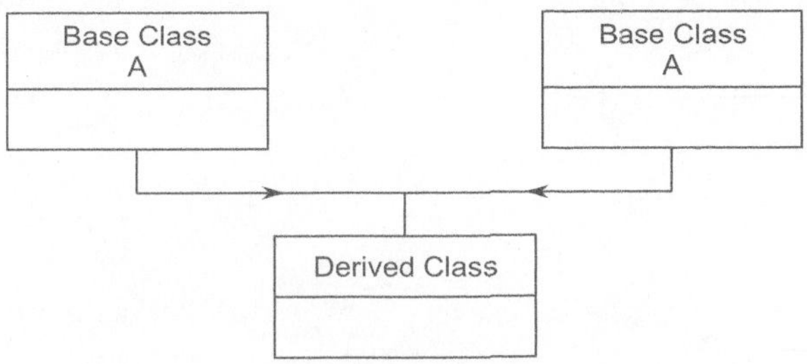

(Multilevel Inheritance)

Multiple inheritance has the added advantage which allows the programmer to mix data/information from more than one source (base class). But the programmer should avoid complexity in the program and should not to inherit from many a class the methods and attributes.

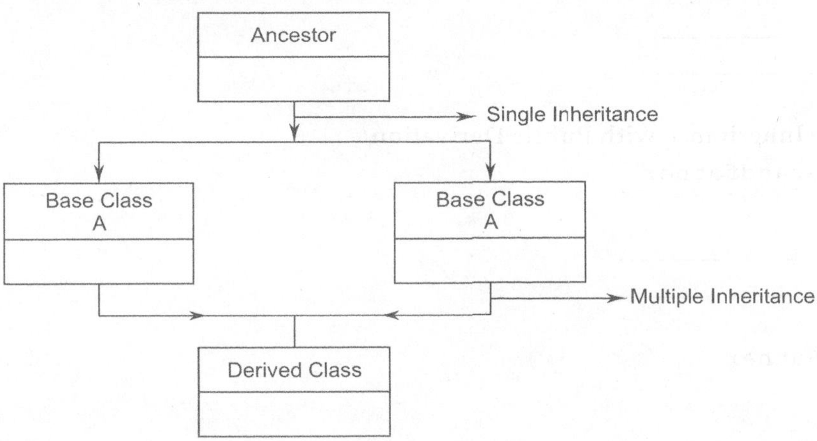

(Multilevel Inheritance)

The following program segment illustrates multiple inheritance:

```
class Grandfather
{
    ____________________
    ____________________
};
class Father
```

```
{
    ____________________
    ____________________
};
class Son : public Grandfather, public Father
{
};
```

Multiple inheritance may be of following derivatives:

1. Private
2. Public
3. Mixed

1. **Multiple Inheritance with Private Derivation class Grandfather**

```
{
    ________________
    ________________
};
class Father
{
    _____________
    _____________
};
class Child : private Grandfather, private Father
{
    _______________
    _______________
};
```

2. **Multiple Inheritance with Public Derivation**

```
class Grandfather
{
    _________________
    _________________
};
class Father
{
    _________________
    _________________
};
class Child : public Grandfather, public Father
{
    __________________
    __________________
};
```

3. **Multiple Inheritance with Mixed Derivation**

```
class Grandfather
{
   ____________________
   ____________________
};
class Father
{
   ____________________
   ____________________
};
class Son : private Grandfather, public Father
{
   ____________________
   ____________________
};
```

Illustration: *Write a C++ program which demonstrates multiple inheritance.*

Solution:

```
//This Program demonstrates multiple inheritance.
#include<iostream.h>
#include<math.h>
class Grandfather
{
   protected:
   int a;
   public:
   void input_a();
};
class Father
{
   protected:
   int b;
   public:
   void input_b();
};
class Child : public Grandfather, public Father
{
   public:
```

```
    void outputdata();
};
void Grandfather::input_a(int i)
{
    a=i;
}
void Father::input_b(int j)
{
    b=j;
}
void Child::outputdata(void)
{
    cout<<"\The value of a is "<<a;
    cout<<"\The value of b is "<<b;
    cout<<"\The value of product a*b is "<<a*b;
}
main()
{
    Child x;
          x.input_a(50);
          x.input_b(25);
          x.outputdata();
}
```

The output of the program will be 1250.

NESTING OF CLASSES

You have so far studied the mechanism of inheritance that a derived class inherits the properties from its base class. There is another way of inheriting properties of one class by another. As per this way an object is supposed to be a collection of many other objects. A Class may contain objects of other classes as its members.

The following program segment illustrates the nesting of classes:

```
class Grandfather
{
    ___________________
    ___________________
};
class Father
{
```

```
     ____________________
     ____________________
};
class Child
{
     ______________________
     ______________________
};
class nested
{
   private:
   Grandfather x;           //x is an object of Grandfather Class
   Father y:                //y is an object of Father Class
   public:
      member functions
};
```

In the above program, it is to be noted that all objects of child class will contain the objects *x* and *y*. This relationship is called Nesting (containership).

Creation of an object containing another object is different than that the creation of solely independent object. An object, independent in nature is created by its constructor. The nested object is created in two steps.

In first step, the member objects are created by constructors. In second step other ordinary members are created.

```
class Child
{
   Grandfather x;
   Father y;                  //member objects
public:.
Child(argument-list): x(argument list1), y(argument list2)
{
}
};
```

In the above program segment the constructors require arguments in the creation of the act.

SOME MORE WORKED-OUT EXAMPLES

1. Consider the following declarations and answer the questions given below:

```
class WORLD
{
```

```
    int H;
    protected:
    int S;
    public:
      void INPUT(int);
      void OUTPUT();
};
class COUNTRY : private WORLD
{
      int T;
    protected:
      int U:
    public:
      void INDATA(int,int);
      void OUTDATA();
};
    int M;
    public:
    void DISPLAY(void)
};
```

(*i*) Name the base class and derived class of the class COUNTRY.

(*ii*) Name the data member(s) that can be accessed from function DISPLAY().

(*iii*) Name the member function(s), which can be accessed from the objects of class STATE.

(*iv*) Is the member function OUTPUT() accessible by the objects of the class COUNTRY?

Solution:

(*i*) Base class of COUNTRY is WORLD
Derived Class of COUNTRY is STATE

(*ii*) Data Members accessible from DISPLAY() are M and U.

(*iii*) Member functions accessible from objects of class are:

- (*a*) DISPLAY()
- (*b*) INDATA()
- (*c*) OUTDATA()

(*iv*) OUTPUT() is not accessible by the objects of the class COUNTRY.

2. Define a class employee with the following specification:

Private members of class employee:

EMPNO	Integer
ENAME	20 character
BASIC, HRA, DA	float
NETPAY	float

Calculate() A function to find BASIC+HRA+DA with float return type.

Public members of class employee:

HAVEDATA() function to accept values of EMPNAME, ENAME, BASIC, HRA, DA and invoke calculate NETPAY().

DISPDATA() function to display all the data members on the screen.

Program.

```
#include<iostream.h>
#include<conio.h>
#include<math.h>
class employee
{
   private:
      int EMPNO;
      char ENAME[20];
   float BASIC;
   float HRA;
   float DA;
   float NETPAY;
   float calculate()
   {
      return (BASIC+HRA+DA);
   }
   public;
      void HAVEDATA();
      void DISDATA();
   };
   void main()
   {
      employee E1;
      cout<<"Enter values;";
      E1.HAVEDATA();
      cout<<"DATA is:";
      E1.DISPDATA();
      getch();
   }
   void employee::HAVEDATA()
   {
      cout<<"Enter number of Employee:";
      cin>>EMPNO;
```

```
        cout<<"Enter Basic Salary";
        cout<<"EnterHRA";
        cout<<"EnterDA";
        cin>>BASIC;
        cin>>HRA;
        cin>>DA; NETPAY=CALCULATE();
    }
    void employee::DISPDATA()
    {
        cout<<"Number of Employee:"<<EMPNO;
        cout<<"Employee's Name:"<<ENAME;
        cout<<"BasicSalary:"<<BASIC;
        cout<<"HRA:"<<HRA;
        cout<<"DA:"<<DA;
        cout<<"Netpay"<<NETPAY;
    }
}
```

3. Define a class student with the following specification:

private members of class student

admno	integer
sname	20 character
eng, math, science	float
total	float
ctotal	A function to calculateeng+math+science with float return type public member function of class student.

Take() function to accept values or admno, sname, eng, math, science and invoke ctotal() to calculate total.

Showdata() function to display all the data members on the screen.

Solution:

```
#include<iostream.h>
#include<stdio.h>
#include<math.h>
class student
{
    private:
    int admno;
    char sname;
    float eng;
    float math;
```

```
    float science;
    float total;
    float ctotal()
    {
       return (eng+math+science);
    }
    public:
    void Take();
    void Showdata();
};
void student::Take()
{
    cout<<"Enter Admission Number:";
    cin>admno;
    cout<<"Enter Student Name:";
    gets(sname);
    cout<<"Enter English Marks:";
    cin>>eng;
    cout<<"Enter Maths Marks:";
    cin>>math;
    cout<<"Enter Science Marks:";
    cin>>Science;
    total=ctotal();
}
void student::Showdata()
{
    cout<<"Admission Number:"<<admno;
    cout<<"Student Name:"<<sname;
    cout<<"Marks in English:"<<eng;
    cout<<"Marks in Maths:"<<math;
    cout<<"Marks in science:"<<science;
    cout<<"Total:"<<total;
}
void main()
{
    Student S1;
    S1.Take();
    S1.Showdata();
}
```

12

DATA STRUCTURES: ARRAYS

AN ARRAY

An Array is a fixed-sized collection of finite number of objects, data values that are all of the same type. In other words an array is a collection of data storage locations. Each of the locations holds the same type of data. The storage location is called an element or component of the array. The individual element within the array is called **subscript**. The subscript is the number of elements in the array surrounded by square brackets [].

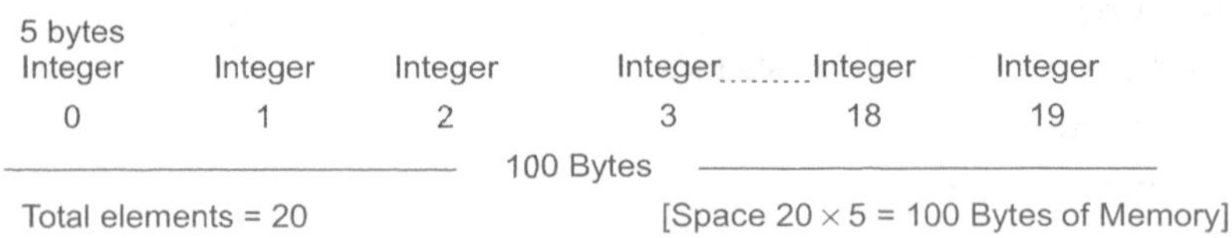

(Declaring an array)

Array elements are counted beginning with 0. In the above figure 20 elements are numbered from [0] to [19].

These elements of the given array are denoted by [0], [1], [2],......,[19].

These elements are stored in continuous locations in the memory. It must be kept in mind that arrays count from 0 and not from 1. The subscript always begins with 0 counting. When the program uses arrays, the array with n elements count from Array name |0| to Array name [*n*–1]. Array name[*n*] will not exist here.

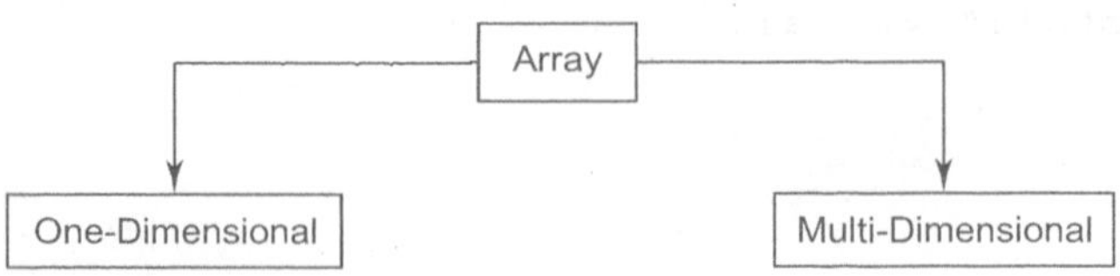

An array may be one-dimensional or multi-dimensional depending upon the specification of elements. If the elements are specified by a single subscript, the array is one-Dimensional and if elements are specified by two or more than two subscripts, the array is called Multi-Dimensional.

One-Dimensional Array

As defined in the previous article, in one-dimensional array the elements are specified by a single subscript.

Illustration: Suppose the number of all 25 houses of LIC Colony are to be grouped. The array may be named as House_number. The components of the array house_number are

house_number [0], house_number [1]...........house_number [24]

These elements are single subscripted because each of the elements has single subscript.

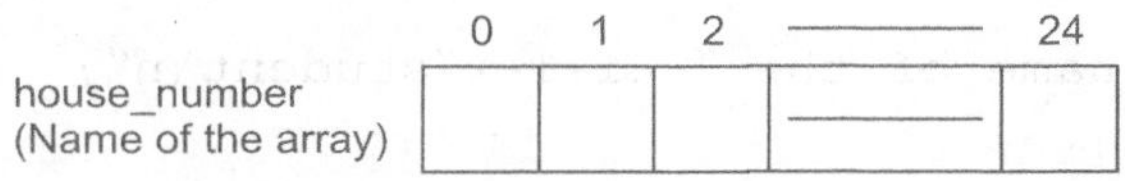

Declaration of One-Dimensional Array

Various terms used in the declaration of one-dimensional array are given here under:

General Syntax—

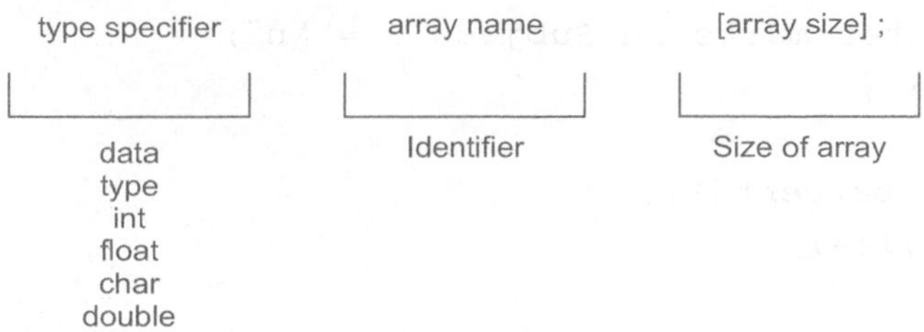

The following statements are one-dimensional array declaration.

int house_number[25];
char letter[12];
float price[10];

C++ allows the declaration of more than one arrays on a single line but these arrays should belong to same data_type and each array be separated by comma.

int a[20], b[12], c[15];

Illustration: *Write a program to store the names of 10 students and their marks in three subjects using single dimension array.*

Calculate the total marks along with percent and display the 'Report' as per given format:

REPORT					
Name	*Marks 1*	*Marks 2*	*Marks 3*	*Total Marks*	*Percent*
–	–	–	–	–	–
–	–	–	–	–	–
–	–	–	–	–	–
–	–	–	–	–	–

Solution:

```
#include<iostream.h>
#include<conio.h>
```

```
#include<stdio.h>
int main()
{
  char name[30];
  int m1[9],m2[9],m3[9];
  int i;
  for (i=0;i<9;i++)
  {
    cout<<"Enter name of the "<<i+1<<"student\n";
    gets(name[i]);
      cout<<"Enter marks in Subject 1=";
      cin>>m1[i];
      cout<<"Enter marks in Subject 2=";
      cin>>m2[i];
      cout<<"Enter marks in Subject 3 = \n";
      cin>>m3[i];
      }
int total [9], percent[9];
  for (i=0;i<9;i++)
  {
    total[i]=m1[i]+m2[i]+m3[i];
    percent[i]=(total[i]/300)*100;
}
cout<<"\t\t\t REPORT\n";
cout<<"Name\t"<<"Marks1\t"<<"Marks2\t"<<"Marks3\t"<<"Total
Marks\t"<<"Percent\n";
for (i=0;i<10;i++)
cout<<"\t"<<name[i]<<"\t"<<m1[i]<<"\t"<<m2[i]<<"\t"<<m3[i]<<"\t"
    <<total[i]<<"\t"<<percent[i];
getch();
}
```

Initialization of Single-Dimensional Array

Initialization as the name suggests means assigning initial values to the elements of array. Array can be initialized only after it is declared. After the array name equal sign (=) can be put and a list of comma-separated values is written within the braces.

General Syntax—

type-specifier array name [array size]=(initial data values};

Example

(*i*) int array[8] = {5, 10, 15, 20, 25, 30, 35, 40};

(*ii*) char vowels[5] = {a, e, i, o, u};

The program cannot initialize more than declared elements for the array.

int house_number[5]; = {3083, 3084, 3085, 3086, 3087, 3088};

The above line produces an compiler error because 6 values instead of 5 have been initialized.

Multi-Dimensional Arrays

Arrays having more than one dimensions are called Multi-Dimensional Arrays. An Array having 2 dimensions is called Two-Dimensional Array.

Two-dimensional array contains 2 subscripts and

Three-dimensional array contains 3 subscripts and so on.

General Syntax—

type-specifier array name [*a*] [*b*] ...[for two-dimensional array]

type-specifier array name [*a*] [*b*] [*c*] ...[for multi-dimensional array]

In the above figure, the declaration of array can be

SquareBoard [5] [5];

This program can also be written as

SquareBoard[25]; as one-dimensional

The number of dimensions *a*, *b*, *c*.......given to an array depends on system to system. Mostly one-dimensional or two-dimensional arrays are used instead of three-dimensional or four-dimensional arrays due to memory constraints.

Initialization of Multi-Dimensional Arrays

Like one-dimensional arrays, two-dimensional or multi-dimensional arrays can also be initialized. The general rule of initializing the multi-dimensional arrays is similar to that of one-dimensional array.

Syntax—

type-specifier array name [row side][columns]={initial data values};

Example int marks[2] [4] = {10, 12, 13, 14, 15, 16, 17, 18};

For more clarity, the program can group the initialization

int marks[2][4] = {{10, 12), {13, 14), {15, 16), {17, 18}};

The inner braces are ignored by the compiler.

SOME MORE WORKED-OUT EXAMPLES

1. A cricket kit supplier in Jalandhar sells Bats, Wickets, Pads and Balls. Write a program in Basic or C++ to generate a Sales Bill using the format given below. Inputs from the console are date of purchase, name of the buyer, price of each item and quantity of each item.

   Calculate the total sale amount and add 17.5% sales tax if total sale amount more than Rs. 3,000.00, add 12% if total sale amount is greater than Rs. 1,500.00 and add 7% if otherwise. Giving the name of the buyer and the date of purchase, display the output as follows:

ITEM	PRICE	QUANTITY	AMOUNT
⋮	⋮	⋮	⋮
			....
		Total	....
		+ Sales tax @	....
		Grand Total	....

Program in C++

```
#include<iostream.h>
#include<conio.h>
#include<graphics.h>
#include<stdio.h>
void main()
{
    clrscr();
    char Name[20], Item[10], Ans;
    float Price, Quan, Sale, TotSale=0;
    int char date[10]; R=9;
    do
    {
        cout<<"\n Enter name of buyer";
        cin.getline(Name, 20);
        cout<<"\n Enter name of item";
        gets(Item);
        cout<<"\n Enter date of purchase";
        gets(date):
        cout<<"\n Enter price and Quantity";
        cin>>Price>>Quan;
        Sale=Price*Quan;
```

```
    gotoxy(5,15);
    cout<<"\n Cricket Kit Supplier";
    gotoxy(7,15);
    cout<<"\n Date of Purchase";
    gotoxy(10,10);
    cout<<"\n Item";
    gotoxy(10,13);
    cout<<"\n Price;;
    gotoxy(10,16);
    cout<<"\n Quantity";
    gotoxy(10, 20);
    cout<<"\n Amount";
    gotoxy(R,5);
    cout<<Item;
    gotoxy(R,12);
    cout<<Price;
    gotoxy(R,20);
    cout<<Quan;
    gotoxy(R,30);
    cout<<Sale;
    R=R+1;
    TotSale=TotSale+Sale;
    cout<<"\n Do you want to continue (Y/N)";
    cin>>Ans;
}
while(Ans= ='Y' | | Ans= ='y');
if (TotSale>3000)
{
    Tax=(17.5/100)*TotSale;
}
else if (TotSale>1500)
{
    Tax=(12/100)*TotSale;
}
else if(TotSale<=1500)
{
    Tax=(7/100)*TotSale;
}
gotoxy(20,30);
```

```
    cout<<"Total"<<TotSale;
    gotoxy(24,30);
    cout<<"+sales tax @"<<Tax;
    gotoxy(28,30);
    cout<<"Grand Total"<<TotSale+Tax;
    getch();
}
```

2. Write a program in C++, using arrays:
   (*a*) To store the Roll No., Name and marks of six subjects for 100 students.
   (*b*) Calculate the percentage of marks obtained by each candidate.
   The maximum marks in each subject is 100.
   (*c*) Calculate the grade as per the given criteria:

Percentage Marks	**Grade**
From 80 to 100	A
From 60 to 79	B
From 40 to 59	C
Less than 40	D

Solution:

The data is stored in two arrays, one to store the rollno and marks and the second to store the names of the students.

The array are then read, percentage and grades calculated and displayed.

Program in C++

```
#include<iostream.h>
void main()
{
    int r[100];         //to store the roll numbers
    int m[100] [6];     //to store six marks
    char n[100][30];    //to store names, each name of upto 30 charac-
ters
    int x,y;
    float p,s;
    char g;
    for (x=0; x<100; x++)
    {   cout<<"Enter Roll number";
        cin>>r[x];
        cout<<"Name";
        cin.get(n[x],30);
        cout<<"Marks in 6 subjects";
        for(y=0; y<6; y++)
        {  cin>>m[x][y];
```

```
        }
    }
    cout<<"\n The data with percentage is as follows";
    for (x=0; x<100;x++)
    {   cout<< r[x];
        cout<< n[x];
        s=0;
        for(y=0;y<6;y++)
        {  s=s+m[x][y];
        }
           p=s/7;
           if (p>=80 && p<=79)
           g='B';
           else if (p>=40 && p<=59)
           g='C';
    else
    g='D';
    cout<<p<<g;
    }
}   //end of main()
```

3. (*a*) Using a C++ program, create a 3 × 3 matrix and store the natural numbers in it row-wise.

   e.g.,

1	2	3
4	5	6
7	8	9

   Now write a program to print the following output:

   (*i*) Sum of the numbers in each row.

   (*ii*) Sum of the numbers in each column.

   (*iii*) Sum of the numbers in left diagonal.

   (*iv*) Sum of the numbers in right diagonal.

   (*b*) Differentiate between subscript and subscript variable.

Solution:

The first nine natural numbers are to be generated using a loop and the values are to be stored in a double dimensional array.

Using 4 different loops the various sums are to be calculated.

For calculating the row and column totals, the procedure is simple, each row and column are totaled and the sum displayed.

For calculating the left diagonal - if the row and column subscripts of an element are equal, then those elements are summed.

For calculating the right diagonal - if the row and column subscripts of an element add up to 2, they are summed.

Program in C++

```
#include<iostream.h>
void main()
{
    int a[3][3], x, y, z, s;
    z=1;
    for(x=0; x<3; x++)
    for(y=0; y<3; y++)
    {a[x][y]=z;
    z++;}
//The array is now full.
//Finding sum of each row
    cout<<"\n The sum of each row=";
    for(x=0; x<3; x++)
    s=0;
    for(y=0; y<3; y++)
    s=s+a[x][y];
    cout<<s<<" ";
}
//The sum of each column can now be calculated cout<<"\n The sum
of each column=>";
for(y=0; y<3; y++)
{   s=0;
    for(x=0; x<3; x++)
    s=s+a[x][y];
    cout<<s<<" ";
}
//The sum of the left diagonal is now calculated
cout<<"\n The sum of the left diagonal=";
s=0;
for(x=0; x<3; x++)
{   for(y=0; y<3; y++)
    if(x==y)s=s+a[x] [y];
    cout<<s;
//Sum of the right diagonal
cout<<"\n The sum of the right diagonal=";
s=0;
for(x=0; x<3; x++)
{   for(y=0; y<3; y++)
    if(x+y=2)
```

```
      s=s+a[x][y];
   }
   cout<<s;
   }
   //end of main function
```

Illustration: *Two matrices A and B are given as follows:*

$$A = \begin{pmatrix} 9 & 6 & 8 \\ 10 & 12 & 18 \\ 5 & 13 & 15 \end{pmatrix} \quad B = \begin{pmatrix} 8 & 7 & 9 \\ 3 & 11 & 15 \\ 2 & 9 & 14 \end{pmatrix}$$

Write a program to compute and print D.

$$where\ D = \frac{Sum\ of\ left\ diagonal\ of\ A}{Sum\ of\ right\ diagonal\ of\ B}$$

Solution:

```
#include<iostream.h>
#include<conio.h>
int main()
{
  in A[3][3],B[3][3];
  int i,j,k,m;
  float D;
  int left=0;
  int right=0;
  cout<<"Enter First Array:\n";
  for(i=0;i<3;i++)
  {
    for (j=0;j<3;j++)
    {
          cout<<"Enter element of row no."<<i+1<<" and column no.
  "<<j+1<<"\n";
          cin>>A[i][j];
          }
          }
  cout<<"Enter Second Array:\n";
  for (k=0;k<3;k++)
  {
      for(m=0;m<3;m++)
      {
```

```
cout<<'Enter element of row no."<<k+1<<"and column no. "<<m+1<<"\n";
          cin>>B[k][m];
          }
          }
for(int p=0;p<3;p++)
{
  for(int r=0;r<3;r++)
  {
    if(p= =r)
    left=left+A[p][r];
    }
    }
for (int t=0;t<3;t++)
{
  for(int x=0;x<3;x++)
  {
    if((t= =0)&&(x = =2))
    {
        right=right+B[t][x];
        }
    if((t= =1)&& (x = =1))
    {
        right=right+B[t][x];
        }
if((t= =2)&&(x= =0))
{
        right=right+B[t][x];
        }
        }
        }
        D=left/right;
        cout<<"D="<<D;
        getch();
}
```

ALGORITHMS FOR ONE DIMENSIONAL ARRAYS

The following basic operations can be performed on the arrays:

1. Search
2. Insertion
3. Deletion
4. Sort
5. Traversal
6. Merge

Search

Search algorithms are of two types:

(*i*) Linear Search (*ii*) Binary Search

Linear Search

In this type of search algorithm each and every element of the array is compared one by one with the given item to be searched.

This technique traverses the array sequentially to locate the given item. This search is called linear or sequential search. Consider the following algorithm for linear search.

OBJECT in Array ARR is having n elements. This algorithm finds the positdon(location) POS of the given item OBJECT. If the search is unsuccessful it sets POS: = 0

The following steps for linear search are explained:

Step No. 1	ARR[n+1]: # OBJECT
Step No. 2	POS: = 1
Step No. 3	Repeat while ARR[POS] = OBJECT
	POS: = POS + 1
Step No. 4	[Search successful?]
	if POS = n + 1, then POS: = 0
Step No. 5	END

Binary Search

The Binary Search is an efficient technique to search the given object (OBJECT) in minimum possible comparisons. In this technique each comparison either locates the position for the object (target value) or divides the array list in two halves. Note that the array list is in order (either in ascending or descending order). The desired element may be present in first half or second half. This technique takes lesser time in searching the element. This is worth-noting that linear search works both for sorted and unsorted elements. This means that there is no condition whether the elements are in ascending or descending order. But in Binary Search, it is necessary that elements should be sorted either in ascending order or in descending order.

The above figure contains n elements and in Binary Search it is divided into two equal parts *i.e.*, $n/2$ and $n/2$.

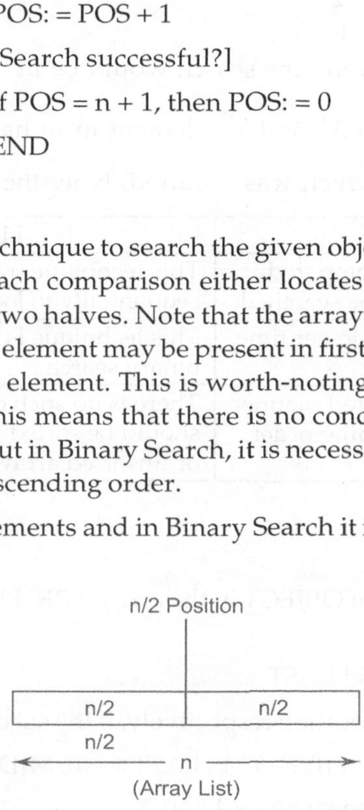

Consider the following example in which the arrays are in sorted form *i.e.*, descending order.

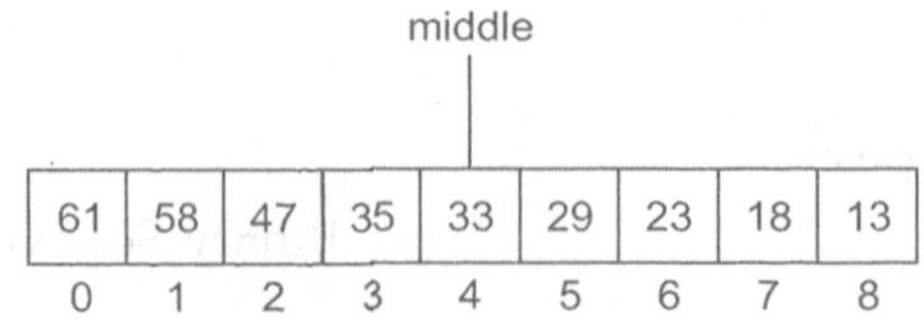

In this case last term = 8

Suppose we want to search for element having value 23 and its location. The following steps are involved in the binary search.

1. Here n = 8. Binary search begins to locate the value at middle. The middle term can be calculated as follows.

$$\text{Middle Term} = \frac{\text{First Term} + \text{Last Term}}{2} = \frac{0+8}{2} = 4$$

   Now the value of 4th location in this array is 33 but the required location is for the value 23.

2. The value 23 lies in the 2nd half.

   Now the second half part is again halved.

$$\text{Middle term of IInd Half} = \frac{5+8}{2} = 6.5$$

   Now 6.5 can be rounded off to 7.

   The 7th element is 18. Therefore, the search would be in lower case (before 7th element).

3. Now split the distance from 5th and 7th element in to hall = $\frac{5+7}{2}$ = 6

   Now the 6th element is 23 which was required. Now the Binary search is completed.

Binary Search	Linear Search
Each element of the array is compared one by one with the value to be searched.	This technique traverses the array sequentially to locate for the given value.
Binary search technique takes lesser time in searching an element.	This technique is slow as compared to binary search.
The elements should be in sorted manner either in ascending or descending order.	There is no such condition that elements should be sorted. Works equally on sorted or unsorted arrays.

Algorithm for Binary Search

Search for location (POS) of the item OBJECT in the array ARR. LB is lower bound and UB is upper bound.

The variable FIRST, MIDDLE, and LAST

denote for first, middle and last location respectively, if the success in insuccessful, it sets POS = 0

Step No. 1 Set FIRST = LB, LAST = UB, MIDDLE = int ((FIRST + LAST)/2)

Step No. 2 Repeat Steps 4 and 5.
while FIRST < LAST
and ARR(MIDDLE) = OBJECT

Step No. 3 If OBJECT < ARR(MIDDLE)
Set LAST: = MIDDLE - 1
else FIRST: = MIDDLE + 1

Step No. 4 If OBJECT < ARR(MIDDLE)
Set LAST: = MIDDLE - 1
else FIRST: = MIDDLE + 1

Step No. 5 MIDDLE: = int[FIRST + LAST)/2]

Step No. 6 If ARR(MIDDLE) = OBJECT
POS: = MIDDLE
print "Successful Search"
else
POS: = 0
print "Unsuccessful Search"

Step No. 7 END

Illustration: *Write algorithm to search 77.5 in the following array ICE[5]*

PRICE	52.6	61.5	71.3	77.5	82.7
	0	1	2	3	4

Solution: The given array is in ascending order: OBJECT to be searched is 77.5

Step No. 1 FIRST = 0
LAST = 4
MIDDLE = int((FIRST + LAST)/2)
= int((0 + 4)/2)
= int(2)= 2

Step No. 2 PRICE[MIDDLE] is 71.3
71.3 < 77.5
then FIRST = MIDDLE + 1
= 2 + 1 = 3

Step No. 3 MIDDLE = int((FIRST + LAST)/2)
int((3 + 4)/2)
= int(7/2)
= int(3.5)
or 3 (rounding off to 3)

77.5	82.7
3	4

Successful search at location No. 3 [location No. 3 means element No. 4].

Insertion

Insertion is a process for adding a new element in an array at a particular place.

The element can be added in an array very subject to space availability.

The insertion can be done in the following two ways.

1. If the array element are unsorted and are not in order, than the new element can be inserted at the end of these elements.
2. If the array elements are sorted and are arranged in ascending or descending order, the new element is added at an appropriate position without disturbing the order of elements.

31	48	96	112	119	141	149	159			
1	2	3	4	5	6	7	8	9	10	

Suppose we want to add a number 117 in this array.

	31	48	96	112		119	141	159		

(appropriate position)

The number 117 will be inserted between 112 and 119 shifting the elements towards right.

31	48	96	112	117	119	141	159		

Insertion

Algorithm for Insertion

Suppose we want to insert an item OBJECT into the array BOOK at the ith position. Assume that the last element is at n^{th} position.

Step No. 1	Set j: = n
Step No. 2	While j > = i
	Repeat Steps 3 and 4
Step No. 3	Set BOOK[j + 1]: = BOOK[j] (shift the element down)
Step No. 4	j: = j – 1
Step No. 5	Set BOOK[i]: = OBJECT
Step No. 6	Set n: = n + 1
Step No. 7	END

Deletion

The process of deletion is just reverse of insertion. In this operation a particular element is deleted from an array. The element, if at the end of the array, can be deleted very easily. The element desired to be deleted is searched by search techniques either by Linear Search or by Binary Search. After the operation of deletion the rest of the elements are shifted one step back. The nth element copies (shifted) to $n-1$ position.

the element to be deleted

Book	11	22	26	29	37	39	48	53	56

Original array

Book	11	22	26	29	37		48	53	56

Element removed

Book	11	22	26	29	37	48	53	56	

Array after deletion

Algorithm

Suppose we want to delete an element from the Array BOOK

Step No. 1	j: = n
Step No. 2	Repeat steps 3 and 4 While j > = 1
Step No. 3	BOOK[j + 1] = BOOK[j]
Step No. 4	j = j – 1
Step No. 5	Set BOOK[i]: = OBJECT
Step No. 6	Set n: = n + 1
Step No. 7	END

Sorting

Sorting is a technique in which the array elements are arranged in a particular order. Simply the order of arrangement may be ascending or descending. In ascending order the elements (number) are arranged from smaller to greater and characters (alphabets) are sorted from A to Z. In descending order the process is just reverse.

12	21	7	55	32	6	18	4	unarranged

List of Elements

4	6	7	12	18	21	32	55

Ascending order

55	32	21	18	12	7	6	4

Descending order

Two very common and popular techniques of sorting are:

(*i*) Selection sort
(*ii*) Bubble sort
(*iii*) Exchange sort

Selection Sort

This is a very simple technique of sorting. Mainly, this technique is used for one-dimensional arrays. First of all, the smallest element is searched and placed in first position. After that the smallest element of rest of elements is searched and kept at IInd position and so on. The first element (in the original form) is exchanged with the smallest element which have been searched. Consider the following example (as shown in the Figures).

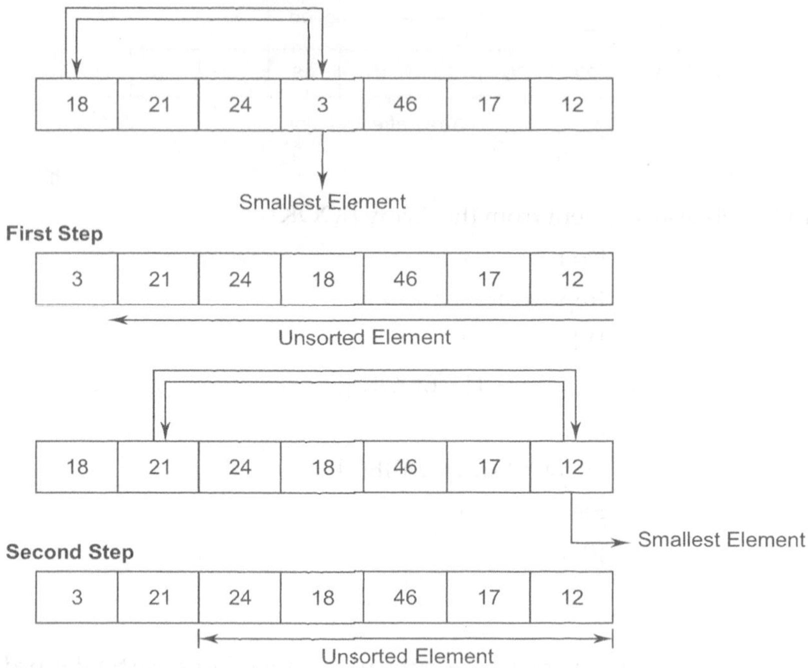

This process continues until all the elements are arranged in an order.

Here the order is ascending one. After all the elements are sorted, the array elements will be arranged as under:

Algorithm for Selection Sort

Consider the following case in which the elements of an array BOOK having n elements are sorted and arranged in ascending order. Variables SMALL and LOC have been used to locate the smallest element.

Variable TEMP has been used to exchange the first element with the smallest element.

Step No. 1	Repeat steps 2 to 7 for k = 1 to n – 1
Step No. 2	SMALL = BOOK[k] LOC = k
Step No. 3	Repeat step No. 4 For j = k + 1 to n

Step No. 4	If BOOK[j] > SMALL)
	SMALL = BOOK[j]
	LOC = j
Step No. 5	TEMP = BOOK[k]
Step No. 6	BOOK[k] = BOOK[LOC]
Step No. 7	BOOK[LOC] = TEMP
Step NO. 8	END

Solution:

Consider the following program which demonstrates Selection Sort.

```
#include<iostream.h>
#include<stdio.h>
main()
{
int BOOK[50];
int j,k,n;
int loc, TEMP, SMALL;
cout<<"\Enter the No. of Elements of the array:";
cin>>n;
cout<<"\Enter the Elements:";
for(i=0; i<n; i++)
cin>>BOOK[i];
cout<<"\Unsorted Elements:";
for(i = 0; i<n; i++)
cout<<" "<<BOOK[i];
for(TEMP=0; TEMP<n-1; TEMP++)
{
SMALL=TEMP;
for(j=TEMP+1; j<n; j++)
{
if(BOOK[SMALL]>BOOK[j])
SMALL=j;
}
if(SMALL!=TEMP)
{
k=BOOK[TEMP];
BOOK[TEMP]=BOOK[SMALL];
BOOK[SMALL]=k;
}
```

```
cout<<"\Sorted Elements are:";
for(i=0; i<n; i++)
cout<<" "<<BOOK[i];
}
```

Illustration: *The following numbers: (89, 20, 31, 56, 20, 64, 48) are required to be sorted using selection sort showing how the list would appear at the end of each pass.*

Solution:

Step I. 20, 89, 31, 56, 20, 64, 48

Step II. 20, 20, 31, 56, 89, 64, 48

Step III. 20, 20, 31, 56, 89, 64, 48

Step IV. 20, 20, 31, 48, 89, 64, 56

Step V. 20, 20, 31, 48, 56, 64, 89

Step VI. 20, 20, 31, 48, 56, 64, 89

Step VII. 20, 20, 31, 48, 56, 64, 89

Bubble Sort

This is also a simple technique of sorting. In this technique, first of all two adjoining elements of the array are compared and if found out of order, these elements are exchanged. After the process is over, the largest element reaches at the end of the array. Consider the following example (as shown in figure).

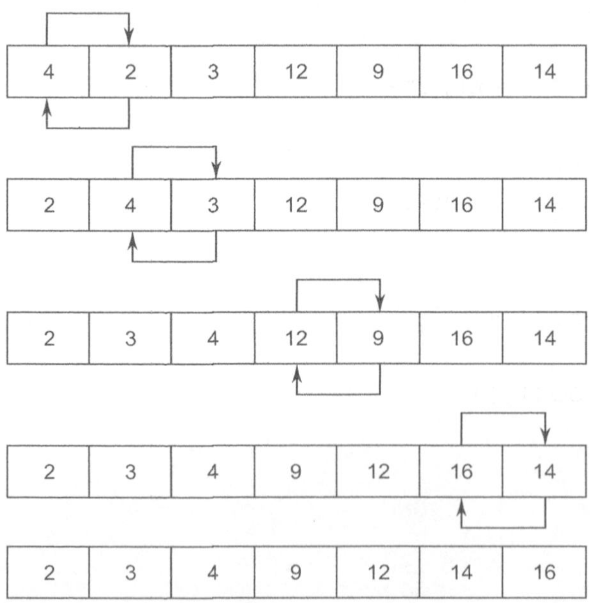

Algorithm

In the following algorithm, the n elements of the array LAXMI have been sorted in ascending order. Variable flag has been used to show the working of exchange in the Array elements.

Step No. 1	k = 0, flag = false
Step No. 2	Repeat steps through 3 to 5
	while(k<n)
	flag = false
Step No. 3	flag = true
	k = k + 1
Step No. 4	Repeat step 5
	for j = 1 to n – 1
Step No. 5	If BOOK[j] > BOOK[j + 1])
	TEMP = BOOK[j]
	BOOK[j] = BOOK[j + 1]
	BOOK[j + 1] = TEMP;
	flag = false
Step No. 6	END

The bubble sort, however, is an easy technique, but the phenomenon depends on exchange and it consumes a lot of time when the number of exchanges is much high.

Illustration: *Write a C++ program to demonstrate Bubble Sort*

```
#include<iostream.h>
#include<stdio.h>
main()
{
int BOOK[100];
int j,k,n;
int TEMP, flag;
cout<<"\Enter the No. of Elements of the array:";
cin>>n;
cout<<"\Enter the Elements:";
for(k=0; k<n; k++)
cin>>BOOK[k];
    flag=0;
    k=0;
while(k<n-1 &&(!flag))
{
    flag=1;
    k++;
for(j=0; j<n-1; j++)
          {
              if(BOOK[j]> BOOK[j+1])
```

```
            {
            TEMP= BOOK[j];
            BOOK[j]= BOOK[j+1];
            BOOK[j+1]=TEMP
            flag=0;
            }
      }
      }
      cout<<"\Sorted Elements are:";
  for(k=0; k<n; k++)
  cout<<" "<<BOOK[k];
  }
```

Exchange Sort

The exchange sort is almost similar to the bubble sort. It also compares elements of the array and swaps those that are not in their proper positions.

The difference between these two sorts is the manner in which they compare the elements. The exchange sort compares the first element with each following element of the array, making any necessary swaps.

When the first pass through the array is complete, the exchange sort then takes the second element and compares it with each following element of the array swapping elements that are out of order. This sorting process continues until the entire array is ordered.

A "pass" means one full trip through the array comparing and if necessary, swapping elements.

Array at beginning:	74	59	66	76	84	81
After Pass 1:	84	59	66	74	76	81
After Pass 2:	84	81	59	66	74	76
After Pass 3:	84	81	76	59	66	74
After Pass 4:	84	81	76	74	59	66
After Pass 5: (complete process):	84	81	76	74	66	59

The exchange sort, in some situations, is slightly more efficient than the bubble sort. It is not necessary for the exchange sort to make that final complete pass needed by the bubble sort to determine that it is finished.

Illustration: *The following program sorts the number in descending order using exchange sort.*

```
# include<iostream.h>
int main(void)
{
    int array[5]; // An array of integers.
    int length = 5; // Length of the array.
```

```
    int i, j;
    int temp;
    for (i = 0; i < 5; i++)
    {
          cout << "Enter a number:";
          cin >> array [i];
    }
    for (i = 0; i < (length - 1); i++)
    {
        for (j = (i + 1); j < length; j++)
        {
            if (array [i] < array [j])
            {
                    temp = array [i];
                    array[i] = array [j];
                    array [j] = temp;
            }
        }
      }
      for (i = 0; i < 5; i++)
      {
          cout << array [i] << endl;
      }
}
```

Traversal

In this operation each element of the array is processed one by one.

Consider the following case, in which the elements are processed in the following order.

ARR[0], ARR[1], ARR[2], ARR[20]

The processing can be on arithmetic operation viz. addition, substraction etc.

Algorithm

Consider that BOOK is an Array and LB is lower bound and UB is upper bound.

Step No. 1	n = LB
Step No. 2	while n <= UB
	repeat steps 3 and 4
Step No. 3	PROCESS BOOK[n]
Step No. 4	n = n + 1
Step No. 5	END

Merging

In the operation merging, two or more sorted lists are merged (combined) to form a single order list. This operation is performed when the size of the arrays is very large. This technique copies the elements of two or more arrays into a new one. In the new array, the elements are merged in sorted sequence.

Step 1

ARR1	7	9	13	18	22	31	33	36	39
	1	2	3	4	5	6	7	8	9

ARR2	8	12	20	25	28	35	46
	1	2	3	4	5	6	7

ARR_NEW

1	2	3	4	5	6	7	8	9	10	11	12	13	14	15	16

Step 1

ARR1	7	9	13	18	22	31	33	36	39
	1	2	3	4	5	6	7	8	9

ARR2	8	12	20	25	28	35	46
	1	2	3	4	5	6	7

These steps continue until the new array (NEW_ARRAY) takes all the elements of both the arrays.

Algorithm

Consider the elements of ARR1[*n*] and ARR2[*n*] as n each and these are to be merged into a new array named ARR_NEW. Ctr1 and Ctr12 are two variables which show. "To be merged" Variables Ctr3 points to the next location in ARR_NEW

Step 1 Ctrl = 1; Ctr3 = 1

Step 2 Repeat Step 3 and 4

while(Ctr1 <= n) and (Ctr2 <= n)

Step 3 if ARR][Ctr1] < ARR2[Ctr2]

ARR_NEW[Ctr3] = AR1[Ctr1];

Ctr1 = Ctr1 + 1;

Ctr3 = Ctr3 + 1;

Step 4 else

[ARR_NEW[Ctr3] = ARR2[Ctr2]

Ctr2 = Ctr2 + 1;

Ctr3 = Ctr3 + 1;

Step 5 While(Ctr2 <= n)

ARR_NEW[Ctr3] = ARR2[Ctr2]

Ctr3 = Ctr3 + 1;

Ctr2 = Ctr2 + 1;

Step 6 while (Ctr1 <= n)

ARR_NEW[Ctr3] = ARR1[Ctr1]

Ctr3 = Ctr3 + 1;

Ctr1 = Ctr1 + 1;

Step 7 END

Illustration 1: *Write an algorithm to find maximum and minimum values of number stored in a two-dimensional array.*

Solution: Let us assume that the size of the array is ARR[10] [10]. Two variables MAX and MIN have been used to store maximum and minimum values of numbers stored in ARR.

Algorithm:

Steps:

1. MIN=ARR[0]
2. MAX=ARR[0]
3. *i*=0;
4. while (*i*<20) repeat steps 5 to 8
5. *i*=0;
6. while (*j*<20) repeat, steps 7 and 8
7. if(MAX<ARR[*i*][*j*])
   MAX=ARR[*i*][*j*];
8. if(MIN> ARR[*i*][*j*])
   MIN= ARR[*i*][*j*];
9. print "Minimum value is=", MIN
   and "Maximum value is=", MAX
10. END

Illustration 2: *An array MARK[40] contains the marks of 40 students in a class. Write a function is C++ to count the number of students*

(a) who scored more than 60

(b) who scored below 30.

Solution:

```
#include<iostream.h>
void count(float MARK[40], int & C60, int & C33)
{
C60=0;
C33=0;
```

```
int i;
for(i=0; i<40; i++)
{
if(MARK[i]>60)
C60++;
else
if(MARK[i]<33)
C33++;
}
}
```

In the above illustration a function called count() has been used.

Illustration 3: *Suppose a one dimensional array AR containing image is ranged in ascending order. Write a user defined function in C++ to search for an integer from AR with the help of linear search method, returning an integer to show absence of the number and integer 1 to show presence of the number the array. Function should have array AR and elements N in the array.*

Solution:

```
//This program illustrates the use of user-defined function to
//search for an integer from an Array
#include<iostream.h>
#include<conio.h>
void main()
{
int linearsearch(int AR[100], int s, int N);
int a,i,N;
int element;
int AR[100];
clrser();
cout<<"Enter Number of Elements=";
cin>>N;
for(i=1; i<=N; i++)
din>>AR[i];
cout<<"Which Element to be Search?";
cin>>element;
a=linearsearch(AR, element, N);
cout<<a<<endl;
getch();
}
int linearsearch(int AR[100], int s, int N)
{
```

```
int found=0;
int i;
for(i=1; i<=N; i++)
if (AR[i]==s)
return(found=1);
return(found);
}
```

Output of the Program

Enter Number of Elements: 5

1

3

4

6

7

Which Element to be Searched? 7

1

SOME MORE WORKED-OUT EXAMPLES

1. Write a C++ program which finds the sum of row elements of two dimensional array A [4] [5] containing integers.

   Solution:

```
//This program adds the elements in each row in a given matrix
#include<iostream.h>
main()
{
void add(int AR[4][5]);
int i,j;
    int AR[4][5];
    for(i=0; i<=3; i++)
    {
        for (j=0; j<=3; j++)
        cin>>AR[i][j];
        {
            add(AR);
        }
    }
}
```

```
void add(intAR[4][5])
{
int i,j, sum;
    for(i=0; i<=3; i++)
    {
        sum=0;
        for(j=0; j<=4; j++)
        {
            sum+=AR[i][j];
            cout<<"The Sum of Row Elements is="<<endl;
        }
    }
}
```

Output of the Program

```
2 2 2 2 2
3 3 3 3 3
4 4 4 4 4
5 5 5 5 5
```

The Sum of Row Elements is = 10
The Sum of Row Elements is = 15
The Sum of Row Elements is = 20
The Sum of Row Elements is = 25

2. Write a user defined function named lower half which takes a two dimensional array A, with size N rows and N columns as argument and prints the lower half of the array.

Eg:

	2	3	1	5	0		2				
	7	1	5	3	1		7	1			
If A is	2	5	7	8	1	The output will be	2	5	7		
	0	1	5	0	1		0	1	5	0	
	3	4	9	1	5		3	4	9	1	5

```
void lower_half (int A[5][5], int n]
{
int j;
int k=0;
for(int i=0; i<n; i++)
{
int j=0;
while(j<=k)
{
```

```
cout<<A[i][j];
j++;
}
cout<<endl;
k++;
}
}
```

3. P is one dimensional array of integers arranged in ascending order. Write a C++ function to efficiently search for a data VAL from P. If VAL is present in the array than the function showed return value 1 and 0 otherwise.

Solution:

```
//search from an array
#include<iostream.h>
#include<conio.h>
void main()
{
    int linearsearch(int AR[ ], int n, int VAL)
    //function to search a value VAL
{
    int i,j;
    int element;
    for(i=0; i<n; i++)
    for(j=i+1; j<n; j++)
{
    if(AR[i]>AR[j])
{
    element=AR[i];
    AR[i]=AR[j];
    AR[j]=element;
    }
}
    for(i=0; i<n; i++)
    cout<<AR[i]
    cout<<endl;
for(i=0; i<n; i++)
{
if(AR[i]==VAL)
return 1;
else
```

```
return 0;
}
}
```

4. Given an array named A with following elements:

3	– 5	1	3	7	0	– 15	3	– 7	– 8

Write a C++ function on a program to shift the negative to left and the positive numbers to the right so that the resultant array will look like the

– 5	– 15	– 7	– 8	3	1	3	7	0	3

Solution:

A complete program has been given below:

```
#include<iostream.h>
#include<conio.h>
void shiftneg(int ar[ ], int n)
{
    int i,j,temp,pos=0;
    for(i=0; i<=n; i++)
{
    if(ar[i]<0)
{
    temp=ar[i];
    for(j=i; j>pos; j- -)
    ar[j]=ar[j-1];
    ar[pos]=temp;
    pos++;
    }
    }
    }
void disparr(int ar[ ], int n)
{
int i;
for(i=0; i<=n; i++)
cout<<ar[i]<<"  "<< endl;
}
void main()
{
int a[10],i,n=- 1;
do
{
```

```
n++;
cout<<"Enter the number";
cin>>a[n];
}
while((n<a) && ! (a[n]==0));
disparr(a,n);
sinftneg(a,n);
getch();
}
```

Output of the Program

```
2 2 2 2 2
3 3 3 3 3
4 4 4 4 4
5 5 5 5 5
The Sum of Row Elements is = 10
The Sum of Row Elements is = 15
The Sum of Row Elements is = 20
The Sum of Row Elements is = 25
```

TYPICAL ILLUSTRATIONS

1. Class MyArray contains an array of n integers ($n<=100$) that are already arranged in ascending order. The subscripts of the array elements vary from 0 to $n - 1$. Some of the member functions/methods of My Array are given below:

Class Name	My Array
Data members/instance variables:	arr-an array of n integers
Members functions/methods	
MyArray()	constructor to initialize n=nn and the array arr
void readArray()	reads n integers that are arranged in ascending order
void displayArray()	displays n integers
int binarySearch(int value)	searches for the value in the array using the binary search technique. It returns the subscript of the array element if the value is found, otherwise it returns.

(*a*) Specify the class MyArray giving the details of the void displayArray() and int binarySearch(int value). You may assume that the other functions Methods are written for you. You need not write the main function.

(*b*) What change would be necessary in the method/function binarySearch(int value) if the given array was arranged in descending order.

(*c*) When will the binary search technique fail to work?

Solution:

(*a*) class MyArray

```
{
int arr[50];
int i,n,middle;
int POS;
int first=0;
public:
MyArray()
{
n=nn;
}
void readArray();
void displayArray();
int binarysearch(int value);
}
void MyArray::readArray()
{
cout<<"enter the size of the array:"<<"\n";
cin>>n;
cout<<"\n enter the elements of the array:";
cin>>arr;
for(i=0; i<n; i++)
{
cin>>arr[i];
}
void MyArray::displayArray()
{
cout<<"the array is:"<<"\n";
for(i=0; i<n; i++)
{
cout<<arr[i]<<" ";
}
}
int array::binarysearch(int value)
{
cout<<"enter the value to be searched:"<<"\n";
cin>>val;
```

```
while((POS==- 1)&&(first<=last))
{
middle=(first+last)/2;
if(arr[middle]==val)
POS=middle;
else
if(arr[middle]<val)
first=middle+1;
else
last=middle-1;
}
if(POS>(-1))
cout<<"position of element is:"<<"\n"<<++POS;
else
cout<<"unsuccessful search";
```

(*b*) The change will be made in the following lines:

```
if(arr[middle]>val)
first=middle+1;
else
last=middle-1;
```

(*c*) The binary search technique will not work if the array is not sorted in ascending or descending order.

2. Class ChaArray contains an array of n characters (*n*<=100). You may assume that the array contains only the letters of the English alphabet. Some of the member functions/methods of ChaArray are given below:

Class Name	**chaArray**
Data members/instance variable	
Char ch[] int size	an array of characters size of array of characters
member functions/methods	
chaArray()	
chaArray(char c[])	
void displayArray() void move()	constructor to assign to initialize instance variables to NULL
chaArray(char c[])	constructor to assign character array c to instance variable
void display Array()	to display the list of n characters
void move()	to move all the upper case letters to the right side of the array and the lower case letters to the left side of the array without using any sorting technique Input: t D f s X v d Output: t d f s v X D

Specify a class ChaArray giving the details of the two constructors and the functions, void displayArray(), and void move() only. You do not need to write the main function.

Solution:

```
#include<iostream.h>
#include<conio.h>
#include<stdio.h>
class ChaArray
{
char ch[100];
int size:
public:
ChaArray();
ChaArray(char C[]);
void displayArray():
void move();
{
chaArray::ChaArray()
{ cout<<" " The array size<<"\n";
cin>>size;
for(int i=0; i<size; i++)
{
ch[i]=NULL;
}
}
ChaArray::ChaArray(char C[])
{
for(i=1; i<=size; i++)
{
ch[i]=C[i];
}
}
void ChaArray::display Array()
{
puts(Ch);
}
void ChaArray::move()
int i,j,temp;
i=j=temp=0;
for(i=0;i<=size-1;i++)
```

```
{
for(j=i+1; j<=size; j++)
{
if(islower(Ch[i]))
{
j=size;
}
else
{
temp=ch[i];
ch[i]=ch[j];
ch[j]=temp;
}
}
}
}
}
```

13

FILE HANDLING IN C++

FILE HANDLING

All programs revolve around data. The sole purpose of a program is to process data to give meaningful information to the user. Data in a program is represented by variables or constants. When we store data which is logically related to each other in a file, that file is called a data file.

For Instance:

(*a*) Information about employees of an organization can be stored in a data file. The data could be employee number, employee name, salary, provident fund, House rent allowance etc.

(*b*) Information about students could be stored in a data file which could contain the student's roll number, name of the student, father's name, age, date of birth, class and section in which studying, date of joining the school, marks obtained in examination etc.

(*c*) Information about criminals can be stored in files. The data could be name, criminal history. Even picture of the criminal and his/her fingerprints can be stored in the file.

C++ treats files as streams. What is stream? It is a small river. Data goes into the files as stream of bytes and comes from files as stream of bytes. A stream is a general name given to a flow of data.

The arrangement of data is as follows:

	Field 1	Field 2	Field 3	Field 4
Record 1				
Record 2				
Record 3				

For example

File name: "student.dat"

	Rollno	Name	Class	Section
Record 1	1019	Rajat Sharma	10	C
Record 2	1020	Anita Dahiya	9	A
Record 3	1021	Dharam Veer	10	A

A data file contains information about a group of entities (students in this case) and is made up of records. A record contains the entire information about ONE entity. A record is further divided into fields and each field contains partial information about an entity and is the smallest meaningful part of a file. A field can be further sub-divided into characters which are most or less meaningless.

Why do we use data files?

(*a*) If we do not use data files, data will have to be entered again and again by the user because data is stored in variable and these variables lose data when we close the program or shut down the computer.

(*b*) A data file can be made common to many programs. The same data file can be used by a number of programs.

(*c*) A data file is not associated with any program. It is a result of a program.

(*d*) In a data file we can add records, delete records, modify the data in existing records or view the records.

Data file are of two types

(*i*) Random and (*ii*) Sequential

(*i*) **Random :** A random file contains records which can be accessed in a random manner. This means we can access any record in any manner and in any order we want. If you are on, say the 3rd record of the file and you now want to access the 100th record, you can directly move to that record reading the records in between.

(*ii*) **Sequential :** A sequential file contains records which can be accessed in a serial manner only. They can be accessed in the order they were written. So in this case, if you are reading the 21st record and now you want to see the 98th record, you will have to go through all the records in between.

According to the type of information that a file holds, files can be classified into the following:

Master files. These files contain information that is normally used for reference purpose. The number of record and the data in the file rarely changes. For example students details like roll number, father's name, address, date of birth etc. This data will not change and even if it changes, the percentage of records which will undergo changes will be very less. In this case, data is going to change if the student changes his/her residence. But how many students keep changing their residence?

Transaction files. These files keep record of day to day transactions. The number of records keeps changing constantly. E.g., student's fee payment, marks obtained etc. These details will keep on piling up as the year goes by. Records are added by the day.

INPUT AND OUTPUT MODES

When a file is to be read, we open the file in INPUT mode. If the file is to be written on, then we open it in OUTPUT mode.

Whenever we have to decide which mode to open in, we have to understand that the program is the source of all activities. So when we are reading the file, it means that the program is taking input from the file. Hence, the file is opened in input mode.

CREATING A FILE IN C++

To create a file in C++, the following steps are taken.

(*a*) The file is opened in output mode (as it is to be written on).

(*b*) Data to be written into the file is acquired. Either the data is asked from the user through input device or the data is generated or the data is taken from another file.

(*c*) The data is written into the file.

(*d*) Steps *b* and *c* are executed again and again until we are out of data. (There is no more data to be input).

(*e*) The file is closed.

What do we mean by opening and closing of files?

A file always resides on a secondary memory device (usually a Hard disk, Floppy disk or a CDROM). Data cannot be read by the processor from these directly. The data files have to be copied from these devices into RAM so that the processor can access them. When we open a file, it means that we are copying the file from a storage device into RAM. After opening the file, we use the file as we need.

When the operation with the file is over, we close the file. By closing the file, we mean that the contents of the file in RAM are now copied back to the storage device. In effect it would mean that the file is being saved.

HOW DO WE OPEN A FILE?

C++ is an object oriented language. We use objects to perform a variety of tasks. File handling in C++ also revolves around objects. The classes to which these objects belong to are **`ifstream`** (for input stream *i.e.* reading files), **`ofstream`** (for output stream *i.e.*, writing to files) and **`fstream`** (for both reading and writing). The prototype for all these classes is in **`fstream.h`** header file. (It should be noted that if you include fstream.h, then we do not need include iostream.h file also (for cout and cin).

The objects are created as follows:

ifstream *a*;

ofstream *b*;

fstream *c*;

Here **a** is an object which will used in a program for reading a file whereas **b** is an object which will be used to write onto files **c** is an object which can be used to read as well as write to files.

The objects are now created. But these objects are not associated with any file. We have to associate these objects to physical files existing on disks. This is how we do it:

```
a.open("student.dat");
```

This opens the file student.dat, which is present on the hard disk and copies is contents into RAM. In the program, the file will be used by referring to the object **a**.

Nowhere in the program will we refer to the filename "student.dat" again.

```
b.open("employee.dat");
```

This command opens the file employee.dat. We will now refer to the object **b** when we want to refer to the file employee.dat.

To open a file in any of the modes using an object of fstream class, we have to tell the computer which mode we want to open it in.

For Example

To open the file in input mode

c.open("student.dat", ios::in);

To open the file in output mode

c.open("student.dat", ios::out);

To open the file in append mode

c.open("student.dat", ios::app);

To open the file in all these modes

c.open("student.dat", ios::in | ios::out | ios::app);

USING STRUCTURES

A structure is a user defined data type which is used to group a number of related data items together. These data items can be referred by a single name. The data items in a structure can be of the same type or different types.

Suppose we wish to group a few related data items like a student's roll number, name, class, section and fee together and we want to give the name to this structure as **student**, we can do so as follows:

```
struct student
{ int rollno;
  char name[25];
  int cls;
  char section;
  float fee;
};
```

The words in italics are reserved words, **student** is the name given to the structure. In future, whenever we wish to create variables of this type of structure, we would use this name.

```
student st;
```

Now we have created a variable st which contains all the five components of **student**. The components can be accessed by using the structure variable name with the component name.

```
st.rollno=1019;
strcpy(st.name,"Rajesh Wahi");
```

```
st.cls=10;
st.section='A';
st.fee=412.50;
```

We could also have stored all these values when the structure was being created.

student st = (1019, "Rajesh Wahi", 10, 'A', 412.50);

We will use structures when we have to read from a file or write to a file.

READING FROM A FILE

When we want to read from a file, we have to create a structure which matches the data written in a record of the file, the following command is given to read form the file.

```
a.read((char*) & st, sizeof(st));
```

This means that you wish to read from a file associated with the object **a**. The data being read is to be transferred to a structure variable **st**. The number of characters to be read depends on the size of the structure.

What happens when this command is given.

(*a*) One record is read from the file and stored in the structure variable **st**.

(*b*) The pointer (called the **get pointer**) moves one record ahead *i.e.* if record number 1 was being read, the pointer will move to record number 2. Therefore, if the command is given again, record 2 will be read.

WRITING TO A FILE

Writing to a file needs almost similar steps to that of reading from a file except for the command. The command to write a record to a file is:

```
b. write ((char*) &st, sizeof (st));
```

This means that you wish to write a record to a file associated with the object **b**. The data to be written to the file is held in the various components of the structure variable **st**. The number of characters to be written is equal to the size of the structure.

When this command is given, one record is written to the file (the data to be written will come **st**.). The pointer (called the **put pointer**) moves one record ahead.

CLOSING A FILE

The command to close a file is simple. We use the object to tell the computer which file is to be closed.

For

```
a.close();
b.close();
```

The file corresponding to the object is closed. You cannot use the object to access the file any more. To access the file again, the file needs to be opened again.

Program

```
\\A complete program to write 5 records to a file.
#include<iostream.h>
#include<fstream.h>
struct student{
     int rollno;
     char name[30];
     int cls;
     char section;
     float fee;
};
void main(){
     ofstream f;
f.open("student.dat");
student s;
int x;
for(x=1; x<=5; x++)
{    cout<<"Enter data for student number"<<x<<endl;
     cout<<"Enter Roll Number          ";cin>>s.rollno;
     cout<<"Enter Name                 ";cin.get(s.name, 25);
     cout<<"Enter Class                ";cin>>s.cls;
     cout<<"Enter section              "; cin>>s.section;
     cout<<"Enter Fee paid             ";cin>>s.fee;
     f.write(char*) &s, sizeof(s));
}
     f.close();
}
```

In this program, we knew before hand the number of records to be written. We created an object **f** of ostream class and associated a file "student.dat" with it. A structure variable **s** was also created. The user was asked to input the values for all the components of **s** 5 times and after input the structure was written to the file.

In real life, situation like the above is rarely seen. We do not know in advance how many records are to be written to the file. So we might use one of the following logics:

Write a program to input a number of records from the user and write them to the above file. The input should stop when the user inputs-99 for Roll number.

```
#include<fstream.h>
struct student {
        int rollno;
        char name[30];
        int cls;
```

```
        char section;
        float fee;
};
void main() {
        ofstream f;
        f.open("student.dat");
        student s;
while(1)
{
        cout<<"Enter Roll Number(- 99 to exit)";
              cin>>s.rollno;
              if(s.rollno==- 99) break;
        cout<<"Enter Name ";cin.get(s.name, 25);
        cout<<"Enter Class  ";cin>>s.cls;
        cout<<"Enter section  ";cin>>s.section;
        cout<<"Enter Fee paid";cin>>s.fee;
        f.write((char*) &s, sizeof(s));
}
        f.close();
}
```

Here we start a loop which is an infinite loop. The 1 in the while statement stands for **true**. As it is a constant, the condition is never going to change. The condition is always going to be true. This loop will terminate only if we give a break statement in it. The condition to be used to stop the loop is often given in the program statement. In the above case, the condition was that the loop should stop if the roll number entered is - 99.

So, we enter the roll number first. If the roll number entered by the user is - 99, then we terminate the loop. If the roll number is not - 99, then the user is asked for further inputs and then the record is written.

READING A FILE

When we want to read a file, we would most often not know many records are there in the file. So how do we control the loop? This is done by using a function **eof()** (eof stands for end of file).

b.read((char*) & s, size of (s));

```
while(! b.eof())
  {
        loop body
        b.read((char*) & s, sizeof(s));
  }
```

Here the file being read is associated with the object **b.eof()** function returns true if the pointer of the file being read is at end of file, and false if it is not at end of file. As you already know that in the while loop, the condition has to be true in order for the loop to execute, we reserve the condition by putting a not operator (!) before the function.

Let us now write a complete program to read a data file.

Read the above file and display all the records in a tabular form.

```
#include<fstream.h>
struct student {
  int rollno;
  char name[30];
  int cls;
  char section;
  float fee;
};
void main() {
  ifstream f;
  f.open("student.dat");
  student s;
  cout<<"Roll No\t Name\t class\t section\t Fee\n";
  f.read((char*) &s, sizeof(s));
  while(!f.eof())
  {       cout<<s.rollno<<"\t";
          cout<<s.name<<"\t";
          cout<<s.cls<<"\t";
          cout<<s.section<<"\t";
          cout<<s.fee<<endl;
          f.read((char*) &s, size of(s));
  }
  f.close();
}
```

Read the above file and display the records of all students in class 10.

```
#include<fstream.h>
struct student {
  int rollno;
  char name[30];
  int cls;
  char section;
  float fee;
};
```

```
void main() {
  ifstream f;
  f.open("student.dat");
  student s;
  cout<<"Roll No\t Name\t class\t section\t Fee\n";
  f.read((char*) &s, sizeof(s));
  while(! f.eof())
  { if(s.cls==10))
  {
  cout<<s.rollno<<"\t";
  cout<<s.name<<"\t";
  cout<<s.cls<<"\t";
  cout<<s.fee<<endl;
  }
  f.read((char*) &s, sizeof(s));
}
f.close();
}
```

Read the above file and display the records of all students who study in a class of user's choice.

```
#include<fstream.h>
struct student {
  int rollno;
  char name[30];
  int cls;
  char section;
  float fee;
};
void main() {
      ifstream f;
      f.open("student.dat");
      student s;
      int c;
      f.read((char*) &s, sizeof(s));
  }
  f1.close();
  f2.close();
  ifstream f;
  f.open("stud.dat");
  f.open("stud.dat");
```

```
  f.read((char*) &s, sizeof(s));
  while(! f.eof())
  {   cout<<s.rollno<<s.name<<s.cls<<s.section;
      cout<<s.fee<<endl;
      f.read((char*) &s, size of(s));
  }
  f.close;
}
```

Copy all the records of class 10 to another file "stud.dat". Display the contents of "stud.dat".

```
#include<fstream.h>
struct student
   int rollno;
   char name[30];
   int cls;
   char section;
   float fee;
};
void main() {
   ifstream f1;
   f1.open("student.dat");
   ofstream f2;
   f2.open("stud.dat");
   student s;
   f1.read((char*) &s, size of (s));
   while(! f1.eof))
   {   if(s.cls==10)
       f2.write(char*) &s, sizeof(s));
       f1.read((char*) &s, sizeof(s));
       cout<<"Records of which class?";
       cin>>c;
       cout<<"Roll No\t Name\t class\t section\t Fee\n";
       f.read((char*) &s, sizeof(s));
       while(! f.eof())
       {if(s.cls==c)
           {
           cout<<s.rollno<<"\t";
           cout<<s.name<<"\t";
           cout<<s.cls<<"\t";
           cout<<s.section<<"\t";
           cout<<s.fee<<endl;
```

```
            }
            f.read((char*) &s, sizeof(s));
    }
    f.close();
}
```

Read the above file and copy all the records to another file "stud.dat". Display the contents of 'stud.dat'.

```
#include<fstream.h>
struct student {
    int rollno;
    char name[30];
    int cls;
    char section;
    float fee;
};
void main() {
    ifstream f1;
    f1.open("student.dat");
    ofstream f2;
    f2.open("stud.dat");
    student s;
    f.read((char*) &s, sizeof(s));
while(! f1.eof())
    {  f2.write((char*) &s, sizeof(s));
    }
    f1.close();
    f2.close();
    ifstream f;
    f.open(stud.dat");
    while(! f.eof())
    {  f.read((char*) &s, sizeof(s));
       cout<<s.rollno<<s.name<<s.cls<<s.section;
       cout<<s.fee<<endl;
    }
    f.close;
}
```

ADDING RECORDS TO A FILE

To add records to a file, we need to open the file in append mode. The command to open the file in append mode is

```
f.open("student.dat", ios::app);
```

Where f is an object of ofstream class.

Here ios::app tells the computer that the file is to be opened in append mode. This means that when the file is opened, the pointer will be at the end of the file, so that the new records will be written there. If a file is simply opened in output mode, as we have been doing, then the existing contents of the file are erased and new data is written to the file.

The rest of the program remains the same (when you wanted to write a few records to the file).

Modifying records in a file.

To change records in files (This means to modify data present in existing records), we need to do the following:

(*a*) Open the file in input mode.
(*b*) Open a temporary file in the output mode.
(*c*) Read a record.
(*d*) If the record which has been read is not to be modified, then simply write to a temporary file.
(*e*) If the record is to be modified, then modify the data in the structure before writing to the file.
(*f*) This should go on till the end of the file.
(*g*) Close both the files.
(*h*) Delete the original file.
(*i*) Rename the temporary file as the original file.

Example:

A file "employee.dat" contains a few records. Modify the record number 14 so that the name changes to "Sandeep Sharma".

Now in this file, there is one record to be modified. Record number 14. To find out which record is record number 14, we need a counter which counts how many records have gone by.

```
struct employee {
   int empno;
   char name[30];
   float salary;
};
void main() {
   ifstream f1;
   f1.open("employee.dat");
   ofstream f2;
   f2.open("temp.dat");
   employee e;
   int c=0; //counter for counting number of records
   f1.read((char*) &e, sizeof(e));
   while(!f1.eof()) {
          c=c+1;
          if(c=14)
```

```
strcpy(e.name, "Sandeep Sharma");
          f2.write((char*) &e, sizeof(e));
          f1.read((char*) &e, sizeof(e));
}
f1.close();
f2.close();
system("del employee.dat");
system("ren temp.dat employee.dat");
}
```

In this program, we keep on reading the records and writing the records to the other file. But if the record number is 14, we change the name before writing to the file.

We will now change the situation. We wish to modify the salary of the employees. The salary of those employees is to be increased by 10% who are getting Rs. 2000 or less.

The program is as follows:

```
struct employee {
   int empno;
   char name[30];
   float salary;
};
void main() {
ifstream f1;
f1.open("employee.dat");
ofstream f2;
f2.open("temp.dat");
employee e;
f1.read((char*) &e, sizeof(e));
while(!f1.eof()) {
   if(e.salary<=2000)
      e.salary=e.salary+(e.salary*0.10);
   f2.write((char*) &e, sizeof(e));
   f1.read((char*) &e, sizeof(e));
}
f1.close();
f2.close();
system("del employee.dat");
system("ren temp.dat employee.dat");
}
```

Now we come to the last part of database management, deleting of records from a file. To delete records, the logic is similar to the modification of records. We keep on reading records from a file and DO NOT write the **unwanted records** to the temporary file. In the end we again delete the original and rename the temporary file as the original file.

Let us say, we wanted to delete record number 14 from the file "employee.dat".

```
struct employee {
   int empno;
   char name[30];
   float salary;
};
void main() {
   ifstream f1;
   f1.open("employee.dat");
   ofstream f2;
   f2.open("temp.dat");
   employee e;
   int c=0; //counter for counting number of records
   f1.read((char*) &e, sizeof(e));
   while(!f1.eof()) {
          c=c+1;
          //we write the record to the other file, if
          //the record number is not 14
          if(c!=14)
          f2.write((char*) &e, sizeof(e));
          f1.read((char*) &e, sizeof(e));
   }
   f1.close();
   f2.close();
   system("del employee.dat");
   system("ren temp.dat employee.dat");
}
```

SOME MORE WORKED-OUT EXAMPLES

1.
```
//Program to Prepare Electricity Bill
#include<fstream.h>
#include<conio.h>            //for getch()
struct consumer {
   int consumerno;
   int billno;
   char billdate[10];
   char name[30];
```

```
        char address[30];
        int prevreading;
        int newreading;
    };
    void main() {
    ifsteam infile;
    consumer c;
    infile.open("electric.dat");
    infile.read((char*) &c, sizeof(c));
    while(!infile.eof()) {
        cout<<"\nBill No:"<<c.billno;
        cout<<"\tBilldate:"<<c.billdate<<endl;
        cout<<"\nConsumer No:"<<c.consumerno;
        cout<<"\tName:"<<c.name;
        cout<<"\nResident of: "<<c.address<<endl;
        cout<<"\Previous meter reading:"<<c.prevreading;
        cout<<"\nN w meter reading:"<<c.newreading;
        int units;
        units=c.newreading-c.prevreading;
        float amt1;
        if(units<=100)
                amtl=units*2.75;
                else if(units<=250)
                amtl=275.0+(150-units)*3.15;
                else amtl=275.0+472.5+(units-250)*3.90;
        float mrent=125.0;
        float amt=amtl+mrent;
        cout<<"\nUnits consumed:"<<units;
        cout<<"\nAmount:"<<amtl;
        cout<<"\nMeter Rent:"<<mrent;
        cout<<"\nAmount payable:"<<amt;
        float pd=amt+(amt*10.0\100);
        cout<<"\nPayment after due date"<<pd;
        getch();                 //pause for a key press
        infile.read((char*) &c, sizeof(c));
        }
        infile.close();
        }
```

2. (*a*) Write a C++ program to create a sequential file named SHARE.DAT containing scrip name and opening and closing prices per share as follows:

Scrip Name	Opening Price (Rs.)	Closing Price (Rs.)
ACC	884.00	877.00
BATA INDIA	176.00	176.10
COLGATE CO.	180.00	181.40
GLAXO INDIA	600.00	600.00

(*b*) Upgrade the file to include the following:

SATYAM COMPUTERS	596.50	589.60
TISCO	99.00	95.40

(*c*) Write a program to get a print out of the Scrip names and the average price of each share.

Solution:

```
#include<iostream.h>
struct share {
        char name[30];
        float op,cp;
};
main() {
        ofstream outfile ("SHARE.DAT");
        share s;
        int x;
        char n[] []={"Acc", "Bata India", "Colgate Co", "Glaxo India"};
float f[4][2]={{884,877}, {176,176}, {180,181}, {600,600}};
for(x=0; x<4; x++) {
        strpy(s.name,n[x]);
        s.op=f[x][0];
        s.cp f[x][1];
        outfile.write(char*) &s, sizeof(s)),
        }
        outfile.close();
}
```

Another Part of the Program:

```
#include<iostream.h>
struct share {
    char name[30];
    float op,cp;
};
main() {
    ofstream outfile;
    outfile.open("SHARE.DAT", ios::app);
```

```
    share s;
    int x;
    char n[][]={"Satyam Computers", Tisco"};
    float f[4][2]={{596.50,589.60}, {99.00,95.40}};
    for(x=0; x<2; x++) {
    strcpy(s.name,n[x]);
    s.op=f[x][0];
    s.cp f[x][1];
    outfile.write(char*) &s, sizeof(s));
    }
    outfile.close();
}
```

3. Assuming the class EMPLOYEE given below, write functions in C++ to perform following
   (*i*) write the objects of EMPLOYEE to a binary file.
   (*ii*) read the objects of EMPLOYEE from binary file and display them on screen class EMPLOYEE

```
{
int ENO;
char ENAME[10];
public:
        void GETIT()
        {
        cin>>ENO;
        get(ENAME);
        }
        void SHOWIT()
        {
        cout<<ENO<< ENAME<<endl;
              }
        };
```

Solution.

```
#include<iostream.h>
#include<fstream.h>
#include<ctype.h>
#include<conio.h>
#include<stdio.h>
class EMPLOYEE
{
int ENO;
char ENAME[10];
```

```
public:
        void GETIT()
        {
        cin>>ENO;
        gets(ENAME);
        }
        void SHOWIT()
        {
        cout<<ENO<< ENAME<<endl;
        }
};
void infile.read();
void infile.write();
void main()
{
clrscr();
cout<<Enter Data:";
infile write();
cout<<"Display Data:";
infile.read();
}
void infile.read()
{
ifstream infile(EMPLOYEE.DAT");
EMPLOYEE s;
while(! infile.eof())
{
infile.read(char*) &s,sizeof(s);
s.outputdata();
getch();
}
infile.close();
}
void infile.write()
{
ofstream infile("EMPLOYEE.DAT);
EMPLOYEE s;
char ch;
do
{
```

```
cout<<"Enter Employee Number:;
cout<<Enter Employee Name:";
infile.getit();
infile.write(char*) &s,sizeof(s);
cout<<"Wish to Enter more(Y/N)?:;
cin>>ch;
}
while(toupper(ch)!='n');
infile.close();
}
```

4. Declare a structure in C++ telerec, containing name (20 characters) and telephone number. A binary data file "TELE.DAT" stores data of the type telerec. Write function in C++ to do the following:
   (*i*) to append record in the file
   (*ii*) display the name for a given telephone number. If the telephone number does not exist then display error message "Record not found"

Solution:

```
#include<iostream.h>
#include<fstream.h>
#include<string.h>
#include<stdio.h>
struct telerec
{
char name[30];
int phone;
}
int phone;
}
int record(void)
{
fstream telefile;
telerec buff;
int count=0;
slen;
telefile.open(TELE.DAT",ios::app||ios::in);
do
{
cout<<Enter Name:";
gets(buff.name);
slen=strlen(buff.name);
if(slen!=0)
```

```
{
cout<<Enter phone number:";
cin>buff.phone;
telefile.write((char*) &buff,sizeof(buff);
telefile.flush();
count++
}
}
while(slen!=0);
telefile.close();
return(count);
};
void dispname(long ph_no)
telerec buff;
fstream telefile;
char pname[25];
telefile.open("TELE.DAT, ios::out);
telefile,seekg(0,ios::beg);
while((telefile)) &&(!found))
{
telefile.read(<char*) &buff,sizeof(buff);
if(buff.phone==ph_no)
{
strcopy(pname,buff.name);
}
}
if(found)
cout<<>ph_no<<"belongs to"<<pname;
else
cout<<ph_no<<"not found!;
telefile.close();
}
```

5. A company AXL has the following salary structure for N number of its employees. The company provides DA, HRA, Conveyance and City Allowance on the Basic Salary. The Name and Basic Salary of an employee has to be entered from the console.

Basic Salary (Rs.)	DA	HRA	Conveyance	City Allowance (Rs.)
1000-2000	19%	10%	4%	0
2001-4000	18%	15%	6%	1200
4001-8000	29%	25%	7%	0
8001 and above	37%	36%	9%	0

The Provident Fund is calculated at 10% of Gross salary for all employees.

Gross Salary = Basic Salary + DA + HRA + Conveyance + City allowance (wherever applicable).

Net Salary = Gross Salary – Provident Fund.

Write a program to calculate and print Gross Salary and Net Salary of each employee along with their names in a tabular form.

```
#include < iostream.h>
#include<conio.h>
```

Solution.

```
#include<iostream.h>
#include<conio.h>
int main()
{
    float da,hra,conv,city,basic,gross,net,pf;
    char name[60];
    cout<<"Enter Name of the Employee::\n";
    get(name);
    cout<<"Enter Basic Salary::";
    cin>>basic;
    if((basic>=1000)&&(basic<=2000))
    {
          da=0.19*basic;
          hra=0.1*basic;
          conv=0.04*basic;
          city=0;
          }
    else if((basic>2000)&&(basic<=4000))
    {
          da=0.18*basic;
          hra=0.15*basic;
          conv=0.06*basic;
          city=1200;
          }
    else if ((basic>4000)&&(basic<=8000))
    {
          da=0.29*basic;
          hra=0.25*basic;
          conv=0.07*basic;
          city=0;
          }
    else
```

```
{
        da=0.37*basic;
        hra=0.36*basic;
        conv=0.09*basic;
        city=0;
        }
gross=basic+da+hra+conv+city;
pf=0.01*gross;
net=gross-pf;
puts(name);
cout<<"\n\t Gross Salary \t Net Salary\n";
cout<<"\n\t ________\t________\n";
cout<<"\t\t"<<gross<<"\t\t"<<net;
  getch();
  }
```

6. A file named FAMILY contains the serial number (No), Name(Name), Address (Add), Phone(PH) and Date of birth (DOB) of fifty members of a family.
   Write a program to create the aforesaid file and update it according to the specifications given below:
   A new name is to be added as;

Serial No.	–	51
Name	–	Anugreh
Address	–	132, Sainik Farms, New Delhi
Phone	–	24312143
DOB	–	17/12/2005

Solution:

```
#include<fstream.h>
#include<iostream.h>
#include<conio.h>
#include<string.h>
#include<stdio.h>
struct FAMILY
{
  char name[40];
  char add[50];
  char dob[10];
  int no, phone, n;
  public:
    void inputdata()
    {
```

```
        for(n=0;n<50;n++)
        {
            cout<<"Enter Serial Number of the Member:";
            cin>>no;
            cout<<"Enter Name of the Member:";
            gets(name);
            cout<<"Address of the Member:";
            cin>>add;
            cout<<"Enter Phone Number:";
            cin>>phone;
            cout<<"Enter Date of Birth of the Member:\n";
            }
            }
        void outputdata()
        {
          cout<<"Serial No._"<<no<<"\nName_"<<name<<"\nAddress
_"<<add<<"\nPhone_"<<phone<<"\nDOB_"<<dob<<endl;
          }
          }detail;
intmain()
{
  ofstream f("FAMILY.DAT",iso::app);
  char ans='y';
  while (ans=='y')
  {
        detail.inputdata();
        f.write((char*)&detail, sizeof(detail));
        cout<<"Record Appended to the File\n";
        cout<<"Want to Enter More Record(s)?(Y/N)";
        cin>>ans;
        }
        f.close();
}
```

INDEX